D1217329

Starr Smith's
Southern Scenes

Starr Smith's Southern Scenes

Journeys Through a Lovely Land

by
Starr Smith

RIVER CITY PUBLISHING
Montgomery, Alabama

By Starr Smith

Starr Smith's Southern Scenes: Journeys Through a Lovely Land

Only the Days Are Long: Reports of a Journalist and World Traveler (a memoir)

Starr Smith's World—an international photo exhibit

More than 500 travel columns covering the world—published in many
newspapers and magazines

Copyright © 2001 by Starr Smith. All rights reserved under International and Pan-American Copyright Conventions. Published in the United States by River City Publishing LLC, P.O. Box 551, Montgomery, AL 36101.

Library of Congress Cataloging-in-Publication Data:

Smith, Starr.
Starr Smith's southern scenes : journeys through a lovely land /
by Starr Smith.
p. cm.
ISBN 0-913515-46-9 (alk. paper)
1. Southern States--Description and travel. 2. Southern States--Guidebooks. 3. Smith, Starr. 4. Southern States--Biography. 5. Smith, Starr--Journeys--Southern States--Anecdotes.   I. Title: Southern scenes. II. Title.
F216.2 .S564 2001
975--dc21
00-013242

Designed by Lissa Monroe
Printed in the United States of America

River City publishes books about life in the South. Our imprints include River City, Starrhill, Sycamore, and Black Belt. Our logo is derived from Court Square Fountain in downtown Montgomery, the traditional symbol of our city. The goddess Hebe poses gracefully atop the fountain, facing the nearby Alabama River, symbolizing prosperity and good fortune for all.

Dedicated with deep affection
to these belles still making
the Scene, whose Southern
passports have been stamped—

Sandra Starr Smith Miller
Lois Smith Clover
Sara Jane Wade Kahn
Algie Hill Neill

Contents

Introduction

WHEN I TRAVEL in other countries, I'm sometimes mistaken for an Englishman. While I am an Anglophile in the first degree, and I've spent a lot of time in England both in war and peace, I like to think that I'm the quintessential Southern boy. I was born in Kosciusko, Mississippi, on the Natchez Trace, and I've spent most of my life in the South. I attended military school, college, or university in five different Southern states—Alabama, Florida, Georgia, Louisiana, and Mississippi—and I've traveled for years throughout this lovely land. So this is a Southern love story.

It's not a serious book. Rather, it's a collection of simple little stories about places and people I've known and written about in my many years as a travel columnist for the *Montgomery Advertiser* and for other newspapers, television, and radio. It's a personal report on good times and many adventures.

In these pages, you'll see ducks parade through the lobby of the Peabody Hotel in Memphis, you'll meet a mandolin-playing schoolteacher who loved Appalachia so much that he started his own museum, you'll meet a visionary who turned New Orleans into a visitors' paradise, and you'll visit historic old mansions in Natchez and Beaufort and take a romantic steamboat cruise on the Mississippi River. In the pages of this book you'll smell fragrant azaleas at Bellingrath Gardens, enter the room in Georgia where President Franklin Roosevelt died, learn about early American life at Colonial Williamsburg, marvel at the butterflies at Callaway Gardens, and stand on the balcony where Rev. Martin Luther King, Jr., was murdered. You'll learn about Louisville's Seelbach Hotel, written about by F. Scott Fitzgerald in *The Great Gatsby*, and you'll visit the New Orleans hotel where Truman Capote claimed he was born. There's a story in the book about the Naval Museum and the Blue Angels in Pensacola, and the Biltmore Estate in Asheville. Of course, there's a lot more, but this is a starter—a little something extra, or as they say in New Orleans, *lagniappe*.

FORTUNATELY FOR all of us who live in the South, the beaches and mountains, the historic and romantic landmarks, and the great vacation attractions are all relatively close by, within one or two days driving time, using the interstate highways. I put this book together with the thought in mind that most Southerners, visiting Southern destinations, would travel by car, which is actually my favorite way of going. I like to drive the interstate for the longer stretches, cutting away onto state and county highways and byways as the mood and fancy strikes. Looking back, I think the best trip I've ever had was a journey to California with my then wife, Virginia, twelve-year-old daughter, Sandra Starr, and my mother and father, Mr. and Mrs. Floyd Rowan (Bud) Smith—going by car and visiting the Grand Canyon, Las Vegas, Lake Tahoe, San Francisco, and the Pacific Coast Highway to Los Angeles and the Mexican border towns on the way home. On that long journey, the interstate highways added hundreds of miles of driving pleasure, comfort, and safety.

Much later, when my granddaughter, Trent Miller Milam, was about ten, we made many journeys to Tampa, Washington, and New York. Sometime later, when Trent was older and had become an excellent driver, we traveled with my mother and father to Atlanta, Disney World, Kennedy Space Center, Nashville, and New Orleans.

In the last year of World War II, I was an Air Force officer on the press staff of General Dwight Eisenhower at Supreme Headquarters in London and Paris. Earlier, before Pearl Harbor, as a young reporter, I covered the massive Army maneuvers in north Louisiana. It was at this time and place that I had the opportunity to observe the talent of then Colonel Eisenhower, and to see the unparalleled role that he played in those pivotal war games. Naturally, during his two terms as president, I followed his career with avid interest. Obviously this remarkable man will be most remembered by history for his superb leadership of the Allied forces in the successful conquest of Hitler. But as president, I think Eisenhower will be best remembered for his vision and persuasive influence in the establishment of America's interstate highway system, which began on his watch and now bears his name.

This 50,000-mile network of four-lane superhighways, ironically modeled after the autobahns of Germany, has literally changed the face of America, joining the Atlantic with the Pacific and linking North and South. Just as international jetliners changed world travel forever, these speedy expressways have changed the way Americans live, work, and take vacations. The states that comprise the Deep South are fortunate, indeed, to have thousands of miles of these great thoroughfares passing through on the way to all points in the United States. To most Southerners, these interstate highway numbers have become as familiar as their own street addresses—4, 10, 12, 16, 20, 24, 26, 40, 52, 55, 59, 64, 65, 71, 75, 77, 81, 85, and 95.

One interstate highway or another runs to, or near, all the South's great weekend and vacation destinations. Alabama's Robert Trent Jones Golf Trail, with its eight courses, was planned and built for the most part on the interstate system. Callaway Gardens, the Biltmore Estate, Ave Maria Grotto, Bellingrath Gardens, the Grand Hotel, and Pensacola's Naval Museum are all handy for interstate travelers. The compelling town of Beaufort, South Carolina, the Little White House at Warm Springs, Georgia, the Museum of Appalachia, near Knoxville, and Florida's Silver Springs are less than an hour from an interstate highway. The Deep South is a never-ending feast of exploration and adventure—the little out-of-the-way towns and villages, the roadside fruit and vegetable stands, the friendly people, the sights and the sounds, the days at the beaches, the nights and the music, and of course the South's good-time mecca, New Orleans, at the intersection of Interstate 10 and the Mississippi River.

In a manner like Hemingway's love for Paris, Southerners have two favorite towns—their own, and New Orleans. Tennessee Williams once observed, "If it can be said that I have a home, it is New Orleans." As a journalist, I have traveled in more than a hundred different countries around the globe, but I must say that New Orleans is my favorite city in all the world. And in this book I've tried to say so—with love and memories.

Starr Smith, April 2001
Montgomery, Alabama

The Peabody Hotel in Memphis
A Southern Blend of History, Tradition, and Luxury

ONE BY ONE the famous old Southern hotels, once the social and business centers of their unique universes, have faded from the scene: Atlanta's Henry Grady, New Orleans's St. Charles, Jackson's Heidelberg and King Edward, Mobile's Battle House, Nashville's Andrew Jackson, Pensacola's San Carlos, Montgomery's Jefferson Davis, Miami's Roney Plaza, Birmingham's Thomas Jefferson, and many others. Few remain. Yet one stands out today—serene, secure, and superior—a gleaming monument to other times.

It is the incomparable Peabody in Memphis, "The South's Grand Hotel." At no time in its long and illustrious 132-year history has the Peabody stood at the absolute epitome of grandeur as it does today. Few hotels in the world can match it for sheer magnificence, and none can surpass it. Then there is the mystique of the Peabody—that indefinable difference that sets a grand hotel above the rest. The Savoy and Claridge's in London have it, the Waldorf-Astoria and Carlyle in New York, the Paris Ritz, the Windsor Court and the Monteleone in New Orleans, the Peninsula in Hong Kong, and Raffles in Singapore—all have this splendid and inexplicable savoir-vivre. So has the Peabody.

Perhaps much of the famous old hotel's allure comes from its phoenixlike past. If the Peabody stands now as a vibrant and brilliant symbol of both the Memphis of yesterday and a great American city of today, it is due to the courage, vision, and love of place displayed by the remarkable Belz family of Memphis. In 1975 Belz Enterprises, headed by founder Philip and son Jack, purchased the Peabody. For years it had stood abandoned and forlorn on Union Street in downtown Memphis, a few blocks from the Mississippi River.

Six years later, in 1981, at a cost of millions of dollars, the Peabody emerged in all its former glory.

THE PEABODY WAS built in 1869 by Colonel R. C. Brinkley. It was named for his friend, the renowned Southern philanthropist George Peabody, who had earlier endowed Peabody College in Nashville, and did much to help the financially troubled South. William Faulkner visited the Peabody when he came up from Oxford, and it was one of Charles Lindbergh's favorite hotels. Every U.S. president was familiar with the landmark hotel, and Confederate general Nathan Bedford Forrest felt right at home there. Today prominent people involved with Memphis's Wonders international cultural series always stop at the Peabody. When asked about the Mississippi Delta, my old friend, journalist David Cohn, said, "The Delta begins in the lobby of the Peabody Hotel and ends on Catfish Row in Vicksburg."

I first came to know the Peabody as a young boy, brought up from our Mississippi home by my father. Later, as a reporter for NBC Radio covering the civil rights struggle and other Southern stories, I was in and out of Memphis many times, always putting up at the Peabody—until that sad day when the old hotel closed its doors.

Enter the Belz family, and that happy time in 1981 when a guest could once again enter the elegant and stately lobby; walk on marble floors beneath handpainted beamed ceilings, skylights of etched glass, and wrought-iron chandeliers; have a drink at the circular Lobby Bar; marvel again at the Peabody Fountain, carved from a block of Italian travertine marble and adorned with cherubs; and watch the famous ducks, the endearing and internationally recognized symbol of the Peabody, frolic and preen in the fountain. The Peabody was back, again and forever the South's grand hotel.

While Belz Enterprises is a family-owned, Memphis-based, diversified company, it is national in scope and reputation. It is involved in real estate, land development, malls, retail outlets, warehousing, and other hotel and business ventures. It's a highly successful third-generation company with deep roots and a long and abiding interest and civic pride in Memphis. What better way to underscore this spirit of gratitude and affection for the town than by returning Memphis's best-known landmark, the Peabody, to its glory days.

THERE HAS NEVER BEEN a part of Americana quite like the Peabody ducks. The twice-daily parade of the five gaily colored marching mallards, on a red carpet from the elevator to the lobby fountains—to the strains of John Philip Sousa's "King Cotton March"—has captured the imagination of the world. I have watched at 11 A.M. as famed Peabody Duckmaster, the late Edward D. Pembroke, led his charges off the elevator and through a fascinated two-deep line of people to the fountain. At 5 P.M. the route was reversed, also through the line of spectators, and Mr. Pembroke took the ducks (one drake and four hens) to their own Duck Palace on the Peabody's Plantation Roof. The duck parade has occurred like clockwork every day for decades, and still goes on like clockwork, morning and afternoon.

Mr. Pembroke once told me, "We've had film crews from all over the world here to film the ducks. They've appeared on the *Johnny Carson Show*, *Good Morning America*, the *Today* show, and other network programs. They've been featured in *Esquire* magazine, the *New York Times*, and other national publications. They are unique in the hotel business, and have given the Peabody strong name-recognition all over the world."

The tradition of the ducks began as a practical joke. One day Frank Schutt, a long-ago Peabody manager, and his friend, Chip Barwick, returned from duck hunting in Arkansas. Feeling no pain, so to speak, they placed their live duck decoys, which were legal at that time, in the fountain. The idea was an instant hit, and there have been ducks at the Peabody ever since, for more than sixty-five years.

Every day at 11 A.M. and 5 P.M., one drake and four hens march through the Peabody lobby to music by John Philip Sousa. They are descendants of the first marching ducks in the 1930s.

The famed sign atop one of the South's grandest hotels.

Jack A. Belz, president and CEO of Belz Enterprises, has said, "Downtown Memphis today stands as a symbol of a dedicated communitywide effort that concentrated significant public and private resources toward a common goal—that of an economically strong and attractive city. And downtown has become once again the indisputable entertainment center of the Mid-South. This is indeed the new Golden Age of downtown Memphis." What Mr. Belz does not say, but everyone recognizes, is that his fourteen-story Peabody Hotel is the signal tower of this Memphis renaissance—a classic example of how one high-minded and resourceful family has made a difference.

WITH 453 GUEST ROOMS, the Peabody is the largest hotel in Memphis. (There were formerly 625 rooms, but in the interest of luxury, ambience, and comfort, the number was reduced to the present 453.) There are fifteen gracefully appointed suites. Four "Romeo and Juliet" suites offer two-story living rooms, fireplaces, interior balconies, and winding staircases. Afternoon High Tea, in the grand tradition, is served in the lobby. In the crowning days of network radio, the Peabody's Skyway Club, atop the hotel, presented the famous orchestras of Tommy Dorsey, Paul Whiteman, Harry James, and other big bands, broadcast nationwide over CBS radio. The Skyway is now completely restored to its Swing-era art deco splendor, and the big bands are back, in the form of contemporary orchestras.

According to my Memphis friends, the Peabody has the best restaurant in town, the premier Chez Philippe, named after Philip Belz, the Peabody's owner. I consider it one of the world's most beautiful restaurants. Just off the hotel's lobby, Chez Philippe is a three-tiered marvel of only ninety places, highlighted by muted murals of masked balls, mirrored alcoves, and Louis XV furnishings. A harpist plays softly in the background, and one can certainly understand the *New York Times's* remark that a Chez Philippe dinner is worth a trip to Memphis.

While Chez Philippe heads the list, there are other restaurants at the Peabody, including Dux, named by *Esquire*, *Playboy*, and *USA Today* as one of America's best places. Decorated in whitewashed walls of lacquer, Spanish tile, and duck decoys, the 200-seat restaurant is fine for lunch or dinner. (But it does not serve duck.)

Mallards serves outstanding light New Orleans–type food in an informal and relaxed setting. Cafe Espresso is a blend of a New York deli and a Viennese pastry shop.

From the standpoint of facilities and service, I believe the Peabody is now at the very crest of its long tenure as a leading American hotel, thanks to modern technology, state-of-the-art equipment, and sound managerial techniques. It is wise to reserve early for a visit to the Peabody, because it is heavily booked year-round.

For more information, contact the Peabody Hotel, 149 Union Avenue, Memphis, TN 38103. Phone 1-800-PEABODY or (901) 529-4000. Fax (901) 529-4184. Web site www.peabodymemphis.com.

Photo by Starr Smith.

William Faulkner's Rowan Oak
His Home and Personal Oasis

On my first trip to Russia, in the early 1970s, I was asked to participate on a panel about modern American writers for graduate students at Moscow University. I was surprised that the writer who fascinated them most was William Faulkner. It had been ten years since his death and twenty-five years since he received his Nobel Prize.

Those memories came rushing back to me when I revisited Oxford, Mississippi, Faulkner's home town. Like the Russian students, I have always admired and been fascinated by my fellow Mississippian. He was born in 1897 near Oxford and, years later, I was born a hundred miles to the south, at Kosciusko, on the Natchez Trace.

I was in Oxford on this last visit to see Rowan Oak, Faulkner's antebellum home and the scene of much of his life and literary work.

On a blazing hot Mississippi day in early July of 1962, Rowan Oak was essentially the news center of the world, when Faulkner's funeral was held in the parlor of the great old house set amid the cedar, oak, and magnolia trees, just off Old Taylor Road, less than a mile from Oxford's Courthouse Square. When the news broke of his death, a telegram of condolence arrived at Rowan Oak from President Kennedy.

On the day of the funeral, telegrams arrived from fellow writers around the world, including such distinguished names as John Dos Passos and Robert Frost. Bennett Cerf, the famed New York editor, was at Rowan Oak that day, as were Shelby Foote, William Styron, and other strong literary lights. Faulkner's family had gathered, led by his widow, Estelle, daughter Jill, and his brothers John and Jack.

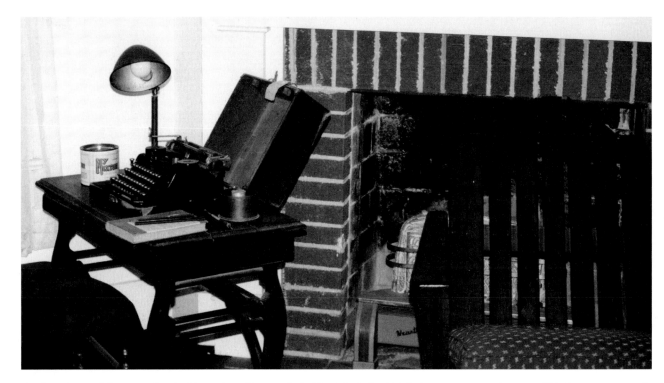

Faulkner's portable typewriter in his study at Rowan Oak. The Mississippi Nobel Laureate typed some of his important novels on this typewriter, including *Light in August*.
Photo by Starr Smith.

Faulkner's black retainers, who had served him so well in good times and bad, were there—and Faulkner's biographer, Joseph Blotner, later wrote that the cypress coffin was opened "so that Andrew and Chrissie Price could say goodbye to Mister Bill, the last ones to look upon his face."

From all accounts, Rowan Oak was the rocklike anchor—the strong, steady, secure mooring—the true and unwavering pivotal point in the last thirty years of Faulkner's life.

THE HOUSE THAT was to become Rowan Oak was built in the late 1840s by an early Mississippi pioneer named Col. Robert Shegogg. In 1872 the house passed on to the Bailey family, and in 1923 it became the property of a Bailey daughter who had married one Will Bryant. In the spring of 1930 the Bryants sold to Faulkner for $6,000 the run-down two-story colonial house. Money was extremely tight in those times, but Faulkner set about restoring the place on borrowed funds.

He gave it not only a new look but a new name. Always the scholar, Faulkner had read that Scottish farmers used pieces of the rowan tree to ward off witches' spells and to bring good luck. Thus Faulkner's new home became Rowan Oak.

Years later daughter Jill told biographer Blotner that the house was "the symbol in Pappy's life of being somebody . . . everybody in Oxford had remembered that Pappy's father ran a livery stable . . . and this was his way of thumbing his nose at Oxford . . ."

Rowan Oak, built in the late 1840s and acquired by William Faulkner as his home in 1930. It was here that he received the phone call notifying him of winning the Nobel Prize. His daughter was married here, and his funeral was held in the parlor.

Photos by Starr Smith.

Dean Faulkner Wells, William Faulkner's writer-niece, who grew up at Rowan Oak with cousin Jill, remembers the ghost stories Faulkner told the children on nights "when foxfire dances in the deep woods around the house, when fog swirls around the trunks of the tall cedar trees, when the old house groans in the wind, and a loose shutter bangs with a lonely sound."

Dean's book, *The Ghosts of Rowan Oak*, was published by Yoknapatawpha Press in Oxford, which she runs with her Alabama-born husband, Larry Wells. In her book, Dean describes Rowan Oak:

> The house stands . . . hidden behind long rows of tall cedar trees . . . it cannot be seen from the street (Old Taylor Road) but at the end of the driveway it looks big and white and beautiful. It looks as if it has been there forever, its two-story wooden frame rising so high that the second-story balcony looks into the very tops of the cedar trees.

Faulkner did much of his best work at the house, including writing *Light in August*, *Absalom, Absalom*, and *A Fable*. Daughter Jill was married in the stately old house surrounded by the farmland that Faulkner loved and cultivated. And one winter's day, in the kitchen of Rowan Oak, he received the phone call from Stockholm that would make him a Nobel Laureate and assure his literary reputation forever.

Rowan Oak is now owned and operated by the University of Mississippi. Admission is free.

The Robert Trent Jones Golf Trail
Alabama's Gift to America's Golfers

ONE NIGHT LAST YEAR I was sitting at the bar of Bud's Jubilee Restaurant in Montgomery. Sitting nearby were two robust men with sunburned faces and giant arms. Seeing the joyful look on their faces, I, being always curious, casually asked why they were so happy. Almost in unison they said, "We're golfers from Louisiana and we're here on a golf safari, and it's been great."

One of them went on to say that they were in Alabama to play the Robert Trent Jones Golf Trail. Another said, "Been here four days. Flew into Huntsville and picked up a car. Played there, went over to Anniston for a round, then to Birmingham for a game, and came to Montgomery to spend the night, and heard about this seafood joint. We like it." They told their golfing story with much relish, and went ahead to say they would go on to Opelika the next day for a round, and then home to Louisiana. They both knew about the new Prattville golf layout and asked when it would open. When I said August of 2000, they whipped out a notebook and said, "It's a date!" They planned, then and there, to come back to also play Dothan, Greenville, and Mobile as well.

Fortunately for Alabama and golfers around the world, that's the way it's been since the Trail opened in mid-1992. Golfers have come from every state and more than thirty foreign countries. The Trail has played host to more than two million rounds of golf, with more than half of the players, like my Louisiana friends, coming from out of state.

ALL OF THIS—along with many other highly successful enterprises and innovations in Alabama—is the inspired and spirited idea of Dr. David Bronner, head of the Retirement

Hole number one at the Judge course. Note the skyline of Montgomery visible on the horizon at left.

Systems of Alabama, which, when he took over twenty-seven years ago, had assets of $500 million. Now the assets total more than $26 billion. Early on, Bronner, an old friend of mine, told me, "I want to do two important things: diversify Alabama's pension fund assets, and also help the state grow and prosper. After all, the stronger the RSA can make Alabama, the stronger the RSA will be." Bronner—a lean, super-bright, free-thinking import from Minnesota, with a background in law and accounting and a Ph.D. from the University of Alabama—thinks no little thoughts and makes no minor plans.

His idea in the late 1980s was to take the popular and growing game of golf and use it to boost Alabama's tourism, to attract retirees, to spur economic development, and, importantly, to stamp a burnishing luminosity on Alabama's worldwide image which, due to opportunistic politics and bad judgment, was in total disarray. Bronner's ingenious idea, combined with his vision, his glorious goal of lasting values, and above all his dynamic personality that inspires others, were the key factors in this giant and far-reaching undertaking.

Bronner, the quintessential entrepreneur, was not thinking in terms of building one 18-hole golf course, but a dazzling collection of public golf courses on eight sites throughout Alabama—and all at one time. Thus later, Paula DiPerna of the *New York Times*, after playing the Trail, and under the headline "In Alabama, Fairways to Paradise," was moved to write, "He [Bronner] has created some of the best public golf on earth, with upscale clubhouses and amenities to boot."

At the start, in his typical "let's get started" fashion, Bronner immediately set about moving his plan along. He was fortunate to get the expert services of Bobby Vaughn, former director of golf at Tanglewood in North Carolina, a man of vast experience and genial personality. The two formed Sunbelt Golf Corporation for the purpose of developing, constructing, and operating the largest golf course project ever undertaken at one time anywhere in the world.

Bronner, well known and widely respected throughout Alabama, helped Vaughn form alliances in all parts of the state and ensured that each site would be built on prime

Dr. Bronner (left), a golf lover, at Troon in Scotland with friends.
Golf Trail collection

land by corporations, private developers, and municipalities. Once this was accomplished, Vaughn, the point man, began recruiting his team of experts, and from that moment on Bronner's dream of building an easily accessible collection of public golf courses combining quality, value, and hospitality was rapidly realized.

This 100 miles of golf course construction—the world's largest—would end up costing more than $146 million. Of course, there had to be an architect. Again Bronner went to the top. He coaxed Robert Trent Jones, Sr., the world's premier golf course designer, out of semiretirement. Jones, with his background of planning more than five hundred golf layouts around the world, came to Alabama, looked the situation over, and went to work with unbridled enthusiasm for the land and its possibilities. Drawing on his reputation of having designed thirty-five of *Golf Digest's* "America's 100 Greatest Golf Courses," it indeed seemed certain that the great master had found in Alabama the land, the water, and a purpose commensurate to his past deeds.

THE LAST OF THE Trail courses, and some would say the most intriguing, is the Capitol Hill course in Prattville. This is the course that I mentioned to my Louisiana friends that night at the Jubilee restaurant. Course developer Bobby Vaughn has said, "We were looking for a centrally located site for our eighth course, and Prattville gives us a facility just one mile from Interstate 65, and only six miles north from Montgomery, the capital of Alabama."

He continues, "Capitol Hill, a fifty-four-hole facility, adds to the uniqueness of the Trail. Because of Alabama's diverse terrain from north to south, the Trail gives a golfer almost every type of golf course layout, from mountains to lakes to marsh to sand. The only type missing from Alabama's Trail has been a Scottish-style layout. Missing, that is, up until the construction of Prattville. The Senator course at Capitol Hill mirrors the famous Scottish-style links courses. There are no trees, but there are more than two hundred pothole bunkers, which are famous to the Scottish design. . . . It is one of the most distinguished courses in the country."

He also said, "The other two championship courses are likewise very different in appearance. The Legislator course rivals some of the more famous courses in North Carolina, with huge pine trees and elevation drops of more than two hundred feet. The

Legendary golf course designer Robert Trent Jones, Sr. (center), flanked by Dr. David Bronner and his wife, Mary Lynn Bronner.

Judge course plays alongside a 200 acre Alabama River lake, with most holes bordering the water, and its breathtaking number one hole tees off over a 150 foot bluff overlooking Cooters Pond and the skyline of Montgomery.

"We are very excited about this facility, and what it means to the Robert Trent Jones Golf Trail and the state of Alabama. We believe Alabama now has the most unique collection of golf courses, public or private, in the world. Where else can a golfer go play a championship public golf facility at an affordable rate, and then get in the car and drive an hour and a half to another facility with the same caliber course, yet different in style, and then do that again six more times?"

The other courses on the Robert Trent Jones Golf Trail are:

Hampton Cove—At Huntsville. The two championship eighteens are a contrast in style and terrain. The short course has eighteen holes.

Silver Lakes—At Anniston/Gadsden. Three championship nines and a nine-hole short course. Water, water everywhere.

Oxmoor Valley—At Birmingham. Two championship eighteens and an eighteen-hole short course. Lots of forced carries and elevated tees.

Grand National—At Auburn/Opelika. Two eighteens and an eighteen-hole short course. Named *Golf Digest's* second-best new public course in 1993.

Cambrian Ridge—At Greenville. Three championship nines and a nine-hole short course that plays long.

Magnolia Grove—At Mobile. Two championship eighteens and an eighteen-hole short course. Scenic lakes, creeks, and marshland carved out of a pine and hardwood forest.

Highland Oaks—At Dothan. Three championship nines and a nine-hole par-3 course. Named as one of *Golf Digest's* top ten public courses in 1994.

The Trail played host to the Nike Tour Championship in 1997 at Grand National at Opelika/Auburn; at Mobile's Magnolia Grove in 1998; and at Highland Oaks at Dothan in 1999. The Buy.Com Tour Championship was played at Highland Oaks, Dothan, in 2000. The LPGA AFLAC Championship took place in 1998 at Grand National, Auburn/Opelika, and at Magnolia Grove in Mobile in 1999. The College National Championship was held at Grand National, Auburn/Opelika, in 2000.

BRONNER'S HOME-STATE newspaper, the *Minneapolis Star Tribune*, last fall paid a sterling tribute to the native son and his golfing masterpiece in a story by Jerry Zgoda and published under the headline "Alabama's Robert Trent Jones Trail Challenges Southern Stereotypes":

> [T]housands of Minnesotans have discovered the late winter/early spring calling of Alabama and the Robert Trent Jones Golf Trail: a collection of eight public complexes that stretch from the foothills of the Appalachian Mountains to the edge of the Gulf Coast. It was envisioned a decade ago by a transplanted Minnesotan determined to change the South's image.
>
> In those 10 years, the traveling northern golfer has watched $100 and $200 daily greens fees become commonplace from the deserts of Arizona to the swamps of Florida . . .

The Media Speaks

Few sporting venues, happenings, or events have received more international media attention than the Robert Trent Jones Golf Trail:

Golf Digest said, "One of the nation's top fifty facilities for service," and "One of the top fifty golf destinations in the world." *Golf* magazine wrote, "One of the top new courses is the Senator at Capitol Hill," and, "Alabama has the American golfer's equivalent of Disney World." *Senior Golf* magazine wrote, "Alabama's galaxy of great courses will change your image of public golf forever."

The *Atlanta Constitution* wrote, "A trip to the Trail is worth every mile and minute spent on the road . . . the finest public golf course in the country." The *Boston Globe* said, "In Alabama, a genius in course design created . . . jewels for everyone to enjoy at one-third the rate of comparable facilities." The *Cincinnati Inquirer* said, "Alabama's 100 miles of golf stands on a par with the construction of the Golden Gate Bridge."

Frequent Flyer magazine wrote, "One of the world's top trips." And, to repeat the *New York Times* bouquet: "Some of the best public golf on earth."

Dr. Bronner playing a tough lie at Bally Bunion in Ireland. Ball is seen to left of Bronner, in flight and slightly blurred.

Bronner collection

The affordable answer for the dedicated golfer is a distinctively different kind of vacation: a trip along rural roads and urban interstates that can begin by smacking a ball through a former soybean field and past an old mule barn near Huntsville in the north, and end 378 holes and 342 miles later in the marshlands north of Mobile.

In between, golfers play through forests and canyons, over ravines and creeks, and onto lakeside promontories on a $145 million project funded by the state employees retirement program and designed to attract tourists, retirees, and industry.

[Alabama has many tourist attractions, but] it's the golf courses, which esteemed architect Robert Trent Jones, Sr., came out of semiretirement at age 84 to create, that attract travelers every fall and spring.

Hobbit Travel in Minneapolis sent 3,000 Minnesotans to Alabama from February to early April this year [2000] to play golf. All 21 trail courses rated at least four stars on a five-star scale by *Golf Digest* magazine readers . . . David Bronner, CEO of Retirement Systems of Alabama, who in 27 years has overseen the state's retirement funds' growth from $500 million to $26 billion . . . [says the trail] has helped double state tourism ($2.5 billion to $5.6 billion) in the past six years. . . .

The biggest price to pay for most golfers on the trail is the devilish work of Jones's designs. Each of the 21 courses has as many as five tee boxes, which, theoretically, allows both experts and duffers to play a course fitting their skills. One hole at the 36-hole Highland Oaks complex in sleepy Dothan—"the Peanut Capital of the World" in the far southeastern corner—has 11 tee boxes and plays as far as 701 yards from the championship tees and as short as 435 yards from the front tees. . . .

The trail's layout—each complex but one is within 15 minutes of an interstate highway and each is within a 2-hour drive of another—allows for several traveling strategies.

You can base yourself in Montgomery, as I did, and be within an hour's drive of 144 holes at Capitol Hill just outside Montgomery; Cambrian Ridge near Greenville, 40 minutes south; and Grand National near Auburn, an hour east. You can stay in either Dothan or Mobile . . . and spend three days playing all 54 holes at Magnolia Grove near Mobile or 36 holes at Highland Oaks near Dothan. . . .

The Trail continues to garner significant attention. In December of last year this item appeared in the RSA newsletter, the *Advisor*:

Microsoft is "the" brand name in computer software around the world. One of their many products, Links LS 2000, is the best-selling golf game of all time. The 2000 game shows Arnold Palmer at Hawaii's Mauna Kea on the cover, and features St. Andrews, Scotland.

Microsoft was recently in Alabama to film the Links in Opelika and the Judge in Prattville. They tell us the Judge will be the cover of the 2002 game, which Microsoft currently sells in excess of three million per year. Microsoft says their intentions are to have two different Robert Trent Jones sites added to the game each year.

Good things started to happen when Mercedes selected Alabama [as a site to build a new vehicle factory], but it is hard to have envisioned that, in one lifetime, Alabama would have Microsoft marketing the Robert Trent Jones Golf Trail worldwide.

DR. BRONNER IS AN avid golfer—moderate off the tee, a sharp short game, and a deadly putter. I told him once, "David, if you were as awesome on the golf course as you are investing big money and building great golf courses, you'd be on the PGA circuit, giving Tiger Woods fits. Bronner smiled and said, "I'm much happier here."

So the Bronner dream is now a reality. Alabama's Robert Trent Jones Golf Trail meanders from the beautiful foothills of the Appalachians in north Alabama to the sparkling Gulf of Mexico in the south. Twenty-one courses at eight breathtaking facilities, none more than a few minutes from a major interstate highway. It is a dream come true, not only for Bronner, but for the people of Alabama, and for golfers all over the world. There is no other place where such a golfing experience is possible.

As *Golf* magazine's Brian McCallen put it: "As travel editor of *Golf* magazine, I've got one of the greatest jobs in the world, but despite my affiliations with the magazine, I'm a public golfer. Sure, I can arrange a game at a private club when and if necessary, but when I'm spending my own dough on the road I look for quality, value, and genuine hospitality. Nowhere do these factors merge in a more felicitous way than on the fabulous Robert Trent Jones Golf Trail in Alabama."

For more information, contact the Robert Trent Jones Golf Trail Headquarters, 167 SunBelt Parkway, Birmingham, AL 35211. Reservations: 1-800-949-4444. Web site www.rtjgolf.com.

New Orleans

America's Favorite—the South's Holiday Mecca

A FRIEND OF MINE was going to New Orleans and wanted suggestions for Cajun music and spicy food. I immediately said Michael's on Magazine Street, home of the exuberant Cajun spirit, boisterous music, fiery culinary fare—and a good place for dancing lessons.

If my friend had asked for culture, sports, jazz, history, a river cruise, a streetcar ride, a gin fizz, Pete Fountain, an aquarium, a voodoo priestess, horse racing, concerts in the streets, a square doughnut, unique cemeteries, Paul Prudhomme, a carriage ride, world-class museums, magnificent hotels, and the finest restaurants in the world, I could have directed him in a flash. New Orleans is like that—a sterling city for all times and all people.

Along with San Francisco, it is one of the most enchanting and popular cities in America. More than twelve million visitors a year come to this big town on the Mississippi River, whose theme song is "Laissez les bon temps rouler!" Let the good times roll!

New Orleans is my favorite city in all the world, over Hong Kong, Singapore, Paris, Marrekech, London, Rio, Barcelona, New York, Lucerne, Sydney, Toronto, and other favorites in the more than one hundred countries I've visited.

I learned about this fascinating old town when I was a schoolboy and traveled down on excursion trains from my little hometown of Magnolia, Mississippi, with a few quarters, an eager curiosity, and a pair of understanding parents. I walked along the narrow streets of the French Quarter, talked to strolling musicians in Jackson Square, admired the paintings on wrought-iron fences near St. Louis Cathedral, rode the old ferry across

the Mississippi River, wrote picture postcards back home, and had my only meal of the day, a Po-Boy at the Pearl on St. Charles Street, just off Canal Street.

IT HAS BEEN SAID that there are only three American cities with an international reputation for superior food: New York, San Francisco, and New Orleans. Many food aficionados, like the late *New Yorker* writer Joe Liebling, used to come to New Orleans several times a year just for the food. He once told me that he had never had a poor meal in New Orleans. Truly, restaurants in New Orleans are judged and cherished like diamonds and emeralds.

Nothing has changed since Liebling's day. In many ways the restaurants are better. The celebrated Brennan clan, called America's First Family of Food, led by the formidable Ella Brennan of Commander's Palace fame, now has several New Orleans restaurants, including BACCO, the Palace Cafe on Canal Street, Dickie Brennan's Steak House, Red Fish Grill, Mr. B's Bistro, and the world-renowned Commander's Palace.

There are at least a hundred first-rate restaurants in New Orleans, maybe more. The great ones with worldwide reputations are, of course, Commander's Palace, Brennan's on Royal Street, the Grill Room of the Windsor Court Hotel, Antoine's,

32

Arnaud's, Galatoire's, Brussard's, and Andrea's in nearby Metairie. There is a relatively new one, Emeril's, which has had a great deal of national attention. And a brilliant newcomer, Lemon Grass, in the International House Hotel, which has, according to *Travel and Leisure* magazine, "The culinary equivalent of perfect pitch."

Other favorites are Felix's for oysters on the half-shell, Mother's for ham sandwiches, the Rib Room of the Royal Orleans Hotel for prime rib and vodka martinis, and for one of the most elegant dinners in the world, the Grill Room of the Windsor Hotel. I always like to drop by the Fairmont Hotel for a gin fizz at the Sazerac Bar, just off the block-long lobby.

Courtyard of the Maison de Ville hotel in the French Quarter, where in room number 9 (to the right of the fountain, with the open drapes) Tennessee Williams finished *A Streetcar Named Desire*.

Photo by Starr Smith.

33

One of New Orleans's legendary streetcars carries tourists down Canal Street, just before turning onto St. Charles.

You can almost hear the music; colorful sidewalk art hangs in the background.

Photos by Starr Smith.

And then there is the Upperline. I recently sent two friends, on different occasions, to Upperline, on the edge of the enticing Garden District. Both came back raving.

I discovered Upperline several years ago, and now I always have at least one dinner there when I'm in town. The restaurant is located at 1413 Upperline Street, phone (504) 891-9822. It's easy to find by car, but if you're in the Canal Street area, a cab is probably the best transportation.

I like Upperline for several reasons. The food, of course, is superb. Another reason is Jo Ann Clevenger, a warm and charming Southern lady, who started Upperline in 1983 and has brought it along carefully to its present pinnacle of international acclaim. At Upperline you see New Orleans socialites, celebrities, and visitors from all over the world, sharing really memorable food. And you see Jo Ann's gracious and special spirit; she is always there with a smile.

I have mentioned many of the great and celebrated New Orleans restaurants. Most of them are not only world-famous and extremely good, but also quite expensive. But you don't have to go to these cafes and spend a lot of money to eat well in New Orleans. There are scores of really fine restaurants all over the city, where you can savor fabulous New Orleans cuisine and not spend a fortune. Look them up in the guidebooks and be adventurous. You won't be sorry. I've done it many times.

Excellent family-type restaurants include the Clover Grill, Poppy's Grill, Seaport Cajun Cafe and Bar, Big Daddy Cole's BBQ, Bagel Works, French Market Restaurant, and, for a taste of elegance for the children, the Court of Two Sisters.

New Orleans, with more than three thousand bars and saloons, is the only American city other than Las Vegas that does not have a closing law. It is open literally day and night. And when the night's party is over, revelers can gather at dawn at Cafe du Monde, on the riverfront, for coffee and beignets.

I TOOK MY granddaughter, Trent Miller, to New Orleans for the first time when she was about fifteen years old. I wanted to introduce her to the city and, I must say, try to recapture my lost youth. That was a few years ago. Now she is a brisk young mother, Mrs. John Paul Milam of Jackson, Mississippi, but she still talks longingly of that week in New Orleans.

A walking tour of the French Quarter is an interesting way to discover unusual sidelights to the city, including the Voodoo Museum on Dumaine Street. Actually the French Quarter, bounded on one side by Canal Street and on another by the riverfront, is a rather small area with a network of narrow streets, quaint buildings, and historic sites. For jazz lovers, one of the most popular venues in town is Preservation Hall, the capstone of American authentic and original jazz.

The French Quarter also has the Cabildo, which once housed the government during Spanish rule; it has Jackson Square, once a drill field, now presided over by the imposing statue of General Andrew Jackson on his rearing horse, the Pontalba buildings, and luxury apartments near Jackson Square, built by the enterprising daughter of the richest man of the Spanish period. There also is the French Market, on a bend of the Mississippi River, graced by arcades and stately colonnades, and home of good restaurants, fine shops, craft stalls, and fruit and vegetable stands.

The Beauregard House at 1114 Charles Street is where Confederate Gen. Pierre Gustave Toutant Beauregard, called "The Great Creole," once lived. The novelist Frances Parkinson Keyes, author of *Dinner at Antoine's*, lived at Beauregard House while writing her celebrated book.

Dakin Williams of St. Louis, an author and a lawyer, autographing his biography of his brother, Tennessee Williams.

Photo taken by Starr Smith at the Tennessee Williams literary festival.

The Gallier House at 1132 Royal Street is a fully restored architectural gem that is an example of how the wealthy people of early New Orleans lived. Lafitte's Blacksmith Shop at 941 Bourbon Street, where the Lafitte brothers sold their smuggled goods, dates back to 1772.

At 632 Dumaine Street is the House of Jean Pascal, called "Madame John's Legacy," reported to be the oldest building in the Mississippi Valley. It is now owned by the Louisiana State Museum.

At the foot of Canal Street, facing the river, is the magnificent Aquarium of the Americas, one of the five top aquariums in the United States, featuring a startling collection of sharks and native Louisiana white alligators, along with sea otters, seahorses, and a vast array of other sea life found in the Americas. Nearby is the Entergy IMAX Theatre.

A driving tour will take you to St. Charles Street, Tulane University, the Canal Street World Trade Center, the Canal Street Ferry, Algiers Point, the Riverside Exhibition Center, Lafayette Square, the Confederate Museum, Lee Circle, the Louisiana Superdome, and many interesting and historic points.

New Orleans was the home, early in their careers, of such legendary writers as Tennessee Williams, Truman Capote, William Faulkner, Lillian Hellman, Katherine Anne Porter, Walker Percy, and others. The Pulitzer prize–winning novelist Shirley Ann Grau, who grew up in Montgomery, now lives in New Orleans.

A family favorite in New Orleans is the streetcar rides. The streetcars of the Crescent City have been internationally famous since the late 1940s, when the unforget-

Bashful beast of burden, covered with flowers, in a typical scene on Bourbon Street.

Everywhere you go in New Orleans, you encounter timeless music for a timeless city.

Andrew Jackson rides again, in sculpture, in front of the St. Louis Cathedral in Jackson Square. The cathedral is the oldest in the United States.

Photo by Starr Smith.

One of the city's many family attractions, the Aquarium of the Americas features marine life from the region.

Photos by Starr Smith.

Higgins landing craft, built in New Orleans, was used in the Normandy invasion. Now on display at the National D-Day Museum.

Photo by Starr Smith.

table Tennessee Williams play set in New Orleans, *A Streetcar Named Desire*, appeared on Broadway and later became an award-winning motion picture. Williams once stated, "If it can be said that I have a hometown, it is New Orleans." On that melancholy February day of his funeral in 1983, the streetcars in New Orleans were draped in black.

Many knowing visitors begin their stay with a streetcar ride from Canal Street out St. Charles and on to Carrollton. It's about thirteen miles and takes an hour and a half. It's a lovely introduction to the city. The "Ladies in Red" are four vintage streetcars, painted red, that run a two-mile route along the riverfront. For more information, phone (504) 569-2700. Ask about an RTA Pass.

Business Week magazine related this adventure, in an article titled "Call It the Little Easy":

New Orleans offers the usual family attractions: an aquarium, a zoo, and a sizable children's museum. There's also the newly opened Jazzland, a 140-acre theme park featuring live music and thirty rides and attractions. More appealing to us, though, were activities we couldn't do elsewhere. One day we took a forty-five-minute van trip out to a wildlife preserve for a two-hour swamp tour that the kids loved. Another morning, my son and husband took a steamboat ride up the Mississippi, while my daghter and I went to a class—on preparing jambalaya, pralines, and bread pudding—at the New Orleans School of Cooking. That afternoon we went on a "ghost tour," a walk through the famed above-ground cemetery that's home to the tomb of a legendary voodoo queen, Marie Laveau.

You'll also enjoy the Audubon Zoo, actually the Zoological Garden, which is one of the top five zoos in America. More than 1,500 animals make their home in the zoo's fifty-eight acres. It's accessible by streetcar, bus, or riverboat, with onsite parking.

So many owed so much to British Spitfire fighter planes, used in the Battle of Britain. On display in the National D-Day Museum.

Photo by Starr Smith.

The Gray Line offers several multifaceted tours, ranging from a Mississippi River cruise on the Steamer Natchez to a tour of the French Quarter night spots. And don't forget the Superdome. There are daily tours from 10 A.M. to 4 P.M. Phone (504) 587-3810. The Superdome, the largest indoor stadium in the world, has played host to more Super Bowls than any other arena, and to three NCAA Men's Final Four Championships, a papal visit, the NCAA Women's Final Four Championship, and a Republican national convention. The Superdome is also the home every year of the Sugar Bowl, one of the nation's premier football classics.

NEW ORLEANS HAS more than 30,000 hotel rooms—all kinds, all types, all prices. More than 2,500 new rooms have recently come on line, including 452 at the Ritz-Carlton on Canal Street in the historic Maison Blanche department store building, and 500 in the Orleans hotels, one on Poydras Street and the other in the French Quarter.

The major chain hotels are present: Marriott, Sheraton, Holiday Inn, Inter-Continental, Royal Sonesta, Hyatt Regency, Radisson, Le Meridien, and the Hilton, where Pete Fountain plays when he's in town. Out stately St. Charles Street in the Garden District is the venerable hotel Pontchartrain, the New Orleans home of countless visiting celebrities. The Westin Canal Place Hotel is on the riverfront at the end of Canal Street, with a marvelous view of the bridges and passing boats.

New Orleans is extremely proud of its small exclusive hotels, mostly located in the French Quarter. Among these are Place D'Armes, St. Louis, St. Anne Marie Antoinette, Maison Dupuy, Maison New Orleans, and Prince Conti. Perhaps the most exclusive and famous of all is the Maison de Ville, where, in room number 9, overlooking the walled courtyard, Tennessee Williams put the finishing touches on *A Streetcar Named Desire*. Because of the Williams connection, and the simple fact that Maison de Ville is a truly great small hotel in an exotic location of the city, reservations are hard to come by in all seasons, especially at Mardi Gras time.

The Roosevelt, a landmark New Orleans hotel named in Teddy's honor, became the Fairmont in 1965, and since then has carried on its grand hundred-year-old tradition in a masterful manner. Widely known throughout the South for the nightly radio broadcasts over station WWL of big-band music from its stylish Blue Room from the 1930s through the 1950s, the old Roosevelt, with more than seven hundred rooms and suites, world-class restaurants and bars, and an international reputation, upholds the Fairmont banner with flair and high fashion. My favorite hotel, the Monteleone, is featured in a section of this book. And the Windsor Court is one of the best hotels in the world.

With a limited amount of land space, and hemmed in to the south by the Mississippi River, New Orleans city planners have become masters of ingenuity and recycling. Dickie Brennan's Palace Cafe is on the site of the old Werlein's Music Store, and the new Ritz Carlton occupies the old Maison Blanche department store on Canal Street. Stephen Ambrose, founder of New Orleans's newest worldwide attraction, the National D-Day Museum, invited me down for the opening on June 6 of last year. I found that it was located, in the spirit of "recycling," on the site of an old brewery along the river. The *New York Times* took note of this ingenious land-use technique, which was carried out with the storied New Orleans style and panache:

> All around the National D-Day Museum, which landed here on June 6, an invasion of art is refashioning New Orleans's once forlorn warehouse district into a chic enclave of culture and condominiums. Old cotton mills and warehouses that stockpiled cargoes from the Mississippi River as far back as the 1830s are being transformed into art galleries, artist studios, lofts, hotels, cafes, and restaurants in an expanding hundred-acre area of some fifty blocks.

New Orleans is a prime city for festivals, notably the Tennessee Williams Literary Festival in March and the Food and Wine Festival in July. I know them both well—attractions of the first rank.

DESPITE ALL ITS modern innovations, New Orleans retains its Old World aura, carefully preserving its history, its reputation for world-famous jazz and cuisine, its romantic Creole heritage, and its commitment to merriment. In an age of medical miracles and spaceships to the moon, New Orleans still loves the moonlight, and retains the joie de vivre that gave it the nickname "The City That Care Forgot."

Recently New Orleans has also become known as the Big Easy. I'm not sure what that term exactly means, perhaps only another way of saying "Let the good times roll."

And it's true that the vibrant old town on the Mississippi has, over the years, become known the world over through its music, food, and ambience.

Yet some remember another town, another time, and, actually, another world. Alvin G. Gottschall, a retired engineer, native of New Orleans, and graduate of Tulane University, remembers New Orleans in another way. In his book *Growing Up in New Orleans*, Gottschall, harking back to the days and nights of the 1930s, writes:

> Movie dates downtown could include stopping in at Napoleon House or the Absinthe House in the French Quarter. After the dances, which lasted until 1 or 2 in the morning, we might go down to the old Morning Call in the Quarter for coffee and powdered doughnuts. I always suspected their cafe au lait had a pinch of Hershey's chocolate in it. This combination really hit the spot. Sometimes we'd stop at Brocato's and get some delicious Italian ice cream—spumoni or cassata. Or we would go uptown to the Toddle House at Carrollton near St. Charles Avenue and have coffee or milk with a nice cold slice of chocolate pie that was covered with a layer of real whipped cream, or visit the "new" Camellia Grill across the street, and have a thick and juicy dressed burger and something to wash it down.

Mr. Gottschall also remembers with nostalgia—and, one can tell, with a certain longing—the dance venues around New Orleans, some of them now gone with the wind: the Beverly Country Club, the Jung Hotel Roof, the riverboats Admiral and President, the St. Charles Hotel ballroom, the Pontchartrain Hotel ballroom, Tulane University gym, and the old Roosevelt Hotel.

Still, with the passing of the years, and a soft transition into another time, the city holds an almost magical appeal to all people, cutting across age lines and constantly offering a wide diversity of attractions. The townspeople live by their own two delightful creeds: "Let the good times roll" and "Lagniappe," which means a little something extra—a bonus. A visitor gets both in New Orleans.

For more information, contact the Greater New Orleans Tourist and Convention Commission, 1520 Sugar Bowl Drive, New Orleans, LA 70112. Phone (504) 566-6044. The New Orleans city web site is www.new-orleans.la.us. In planning your visit, write for a copy of *Where* magazine, 921 Canal Street, New Orleans, LA 70112, a monthly publication that carries an up-to-date list of things to do and see in this most enticing of all American cities.

Weidmann's Restaurant in Meridian
A Family Tradition of Great Food

EARLY IN THE MORNING of July 1, 1935, the news center of the aviation world was a Mississippi town just across the state line from Alabama. The city was Meridian, and that day the Key brothers, Fred and Al, broke the world's endurance record for nonstop air-refueling continuous flight.

The young airmen flew their tiny Curtiss Robin single-engine plane, dubbed the *Ole Miss*, over Meridian for 653 hours and 34 minutes—27 days and nights, a record that would stand until broken by astronauts in 1973.

After the tumult and excitement of the landing, everybody—the world press, Claire Chennault (later of Flying Tiger fame), Col. Roscoe Turner (the colorful speed flier), and other luminaries—went to Weidmann's Restaurant for a victory celebration. Ironically, the Key brothers didn't get their victory celebration until a week later. But that was at Weidmann's, too.

And that was altogether fitting and proper. In Meridian all good things begin or end at Weidmann's—family gatherings, birthdays, graduation celebrations, Mardi Gras suppers, wedding festivals, and all other special times and events in the lives of people. Moreover, travelers in the know from around the nation always arrange their schedules when they're in this part of the country to arrive in Meridian in time for lunch or dinner at Weidmann's, which, over the years, has become a famous landmark.

My mother died in 1997, at age 97. She was born in Mississippi and spent most of her adult life in Mobile. For more than fifty years she had been an aficionado of Weidmann's. My mother passed the last few years of her life at St. Catherine's, a retire-

Since 1870, reads the sign. The landmark restaurant was founded by Felix and Clara Weidmann.

Photo by Starr Smith.

ment home at Madison, just outside Jackson, Mississippi, where her friend Senator John Stennis also lived. Several times a year I would bring her over to Montgomery. She always insisted that the driving schedule be timed for lunch at Weidmann's.

Weidmann's has been in Meridian for more than 130 years. Its life, growth, and phenomenal success have followed closely that of this prosperous city, one of Mississippi's largest.

Gen. Sherman almost leveled the little hamlet during the Civil War, but the rebuilding started almost before he got out of town. It was just a few years later, in 1870, that Felix Weidmann and his wife, Clara, arrived in Meridian by way of Mobile. It is not surprising that Weidmann opened his little one-room restaurant. After all, he had been a chef on the ship that brought him from Europe to America. But despite his determination and dreams, it is doubtful he realized just how successful he would be.

Original Front Room at Weidmann's, with long counter and brass rail. The restaurant serves consistently good food with a charming touch of imagination and showmanship.

WEIDMANN'S THRIVES not on reputation alone. There are more than a hundred items on the menu. And with the Gulf Coast only a few hours away, all kinds of fresh seafood are available.

Freshness is a hallmark of all Weidmann's foods—fruits, vegetables, breads, soups, and dairy products and sweets, especially ice cream, pies, and cakes. Coffee, one of the specialties, is a Niolon's blend that has been coming from the same coffee house since 1883. A Weidmann's signature is a small brown pot of peanut butter and crackers on every table all the time.

Weidmann's doesn't offer haute cuisine in the French manner, but it does offer consistently good food served in a light, cheerful, pleasant atmosphere where a charming touch of imagination and showmanship prevail.

The *Montgomery Advertiser's* perceptive and peripatetic reporter, Alvin Benn, has written:

Gloria Chancellor, great-great-granddaughter of the founders, is now an owner. This photo was made in the Plate Room. Note pictures of Archie Manning, Bear Bryant, Doc Severinsen, and many other celebrities.

Photo by Starr Smith.

> Weidmann's popularity involves far more than just food. Atmosphere has attracted people from throughout the Southeast since Ulysses Grant was in the White House. Recipes are handed down from generation to generation of cooks who have become almost part of the Weidmann family. Waiters don't stray. One worked at the restaurant for about half a century.

In January 1989, Weidmann's passed another milestone when a fifth generation took over, in the persons of Lester "Poo" Chancellor and his wife, Gloria, the great-great-grand-daughter of the founder, Felix Weidmann.

Lester and Gloria bought the restaurant from Mrs. Chancellor's parents, Edward "Shorty" McWilliams and his wife, the former Gloria Weidmann. Shorty McWilliams brought a measure of fame to Weidmann's. He was a football star at both West Point and Mississippi State and his portrait now hangs in the Plate Room of the restaurant.

The McWilliamses ran the restaurant after taking over from Mrs. McWilliams's mother, Mrs. Dorothy Weidmann, widow of Henry Weidmann, who died in 1956.

And though the fifth generation is in charge, things will remain the same, said Chancellor. "We'll just follow the Weidmann tradition," he said. "It's worked for over 130 years." His wife, Gloria, adds, "We have two daughters. There is a possibility that Weidmann's will eventually move into a sixth generation."

TRADITION IS FOUND not only in the food, service, and a long and successful life, but in the Weidmann's fixtures as well. There are three dining rooms—the original Front Room with a counter and brass rail, the Plate Room with a fireplace to the rear, and the 1870 Room, named, of course, for the year Weidmann's was founded.

In the 1870 Room hangs a giant wheel, now a chandelier, from the Mobile river-boat *Peerless*. A large hand-carved Swiss clock from Germany's Black Forest, once owned by the pioneer Threefoot family of Meridian, hangs in the Front Room. An imprint of it forms the menu's logo.

Photographs cover the walls in the Front Room and the Plate Room. There are pictures of the famous and the near-famous who have dined there, among them President Dwight Eisenhower, Dizzy Dean, Jack Dempsey, Ted Williams, Bear Bryant, Vincent Price, Doc Severinsen, Anita Bryant, and all the Miss Americas who have come from Mississippi. Among the photos is that of bandleader Jan Garber, the "Idol of the Airlanes," who began his career playing at Weidmann's. Every Mississippi governor and U.S. senator in the last hundred years has dined at Weidmann's at one time or another.

Sela Ward, the celebrated dramatic actress who has had such great success in television and film, is a Meridian native and University of Alabama graduate. She lives now in California but comes to Meridian several times a year, where she is instrumental in restoring the Grand Opera Theatre. With her husband and two children, she always dines at Weidmann's and they all get a kick out of seeing her photo on the wall. Her family still lives in Meridian, and on my last visit her father was having lunch at Weidmann's.

Perhaps even more impressive than these "Who's Who" photographs is a special wall of photos of young men and boys. These are pictures of Meridian's boys in uniform who have paid the ultimate price of freedom in the service of their country.

But there is one photograph that is conspicuous by its absence—that of Charles Lindbergh. He passed through Meridian once, landing his plane for refueling. A table was set and was ready for him at Weidmann's, but, alas, the Lone Eagle was on a tight schedule and he could not stop to dine, which deprived Weidmann's of a photo for its wall—but which, even worse, cost Lindbergh a great meal.

Weidmann's is easy to find. It's downtown on 22nd Avenue. Coming into Meridian from the east on I-59/20, take the downtown exit and it's just over the bridge on the right. The restaurant is open seven days a week from 6 A.M. to 10 P.M. It closes only two days a year, January 1 and July 4. For information, phone (601) 693-1751.

Tuscaloosa's
Paul W. "Bear" Bryant Museum
America's Greatest Coach and His Team

SEVERAL YEARS AGO, during Coach Paul "Bear" Bryant's series of national championship football teams at the University of Alabama, I received a phone call from a well-known Alabama businessman who was moved by an interview with Coach Bryant that he had seen on national television. I knew my caller well. He had two sons at the University. Although he had never attended college, he was now a successful self-made man.

He said, "I want to give the University seventy-five thousand dollars. They can use it any way they want to. But I want to give it personally to Coach Bryant. I want him to know that I'm giving the money because of him and how much he has meant to me and to this country."

He asked me to arrange this for him, since I knew Coach Bryant and the people at the University. I called Dr. Howard Gundy, acting president of the University. He set up a meeting with Coach Bryant, and my friend and I went to Tuscaloosa.

We met in Coach Bryant's office. He could not have been nicer—all smiles, gracious. The check changed hands and Coach Bryant said to my friend, "Let's get a picture. Just the two of us." That photo is now in an honored place in the businessman's office in Montgomery.

I tell this story only to underscore the fact that the influence, prestige, and value of Coach Bryant to the University of Alabama did not begin or end on the gridiron or with

Bryant's office in a modern re-creation. Note the houndstooth hat on the coat rack and the team photos on the wall. The telephone on the desk, behind the picture frame, is crimson.

Photo by Starr Smith.

national football championships. He touched the lives of people all over America, in sports and out, and, in my opinion, will for generations to come.

Just before Coach Bryant died, noted sportswriter Al Browning was talking with him and mentioned the inspiration and admiration that he brought out in people—how they looked up to him and always would.

Coach Bryant said, "Al, life is not like that. You're here today and gone tomorrow. I'll be forgotten as soon as they put me in the ground." For one of the few times in his life, Coach Bryant was wrong about an important thing.

STANDING TODAY ON the campus of the University of Alabama is the Paul W. Bryant Museum, a tribute etched in stone to the man who was America's most honored and successful college football coach, and one of the most celebrated sports figures who ever lived.

The museum opened in October 1988. On the day of the LSU game that year, more than 3,500 visitors went through the museum. About 300 visit on weekdays now.

Bryant retired as head coach at the University after the 1982 season. He had held the post for twenty-five seasons. A month later, as he approached his seventieth year, he died. Had he lived, today he would be almost ninety years old.

When the subject of the museum was brought up to Coach Bryant before he died, he was emphatic, saying, "This should not be a monument to me. I don't want that. I want it to be a tribute to my former players and assistant coaches, the people who won all those games."

The museum is much more than that. It is both an exhibition hall and sports archive. It traces the history and tradition of Alabama football from 1892, the year the university organized its first team, to the national championship of 1992.

The great triumphant years of Wallace Wade and Frank Thomas as Alabama head coaches are duly noted, and there are numerous items of memorabilia from those times. Coaches Wade and Thomas's trips to the Rose Bowl, where the Alabama football dynasty really began, stand out as the opening moments of the drama that unfolded in all its glory during the Bryant years. The museum lives up to its billing as the showplace for

Bust of Coach Bryant in the museum. He once told a sportswriter, "I'll be forgotten as soon as they put me in the ground."

Photo by Starr Smith.

53

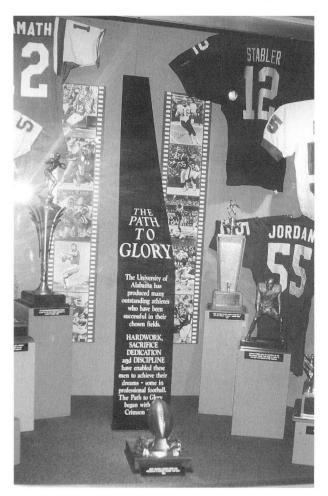

Bryant's reputation helped Bama get some of the best talent. Pro jerseys of Tide stars Joe Namath, Ken Stabler, Lee Roy Jordan, and others.

Photo by Starr Smith.

a hundred years of history of Alabama football.

Coach Bryant's signature honor, winning 323 major-college football games, more than any other coach in history, is only one of the highlights in his brilliant career. He was three-time winner of the National Coach of the Year Award; eight-time winner of the Southeastern Conference Coach of the Year Award; elected Coach of the Century by a media poll in 1979 and Coach of the Decade by the NCAA in 1969; and the first coach since the formation of the NCAA to win one hundred games in a decade. As player and coach, Bryant went to more bowl games than any other person in the history of football.

It's all there in the museum, in graphic and historical detail, from the thrilling picture of the Penn State–Alabama goal line stand in the 1979 Sugar Bowl, which greets visitors in the lobby, to the striking and emotive bust of Coach Bryant—without the houndstooth hat, because he did not believe in wearing hats indoors. There is the Waterford crystal replica of that famous hat; his coaching jacket and other personal items; a re-creation of his office (not cluttered enough); blown-up pictures of his national championship teams; and many other items of memorabilia. Coach Bryant's successful coaching stints at Maryland, Kentucky, and Texas A&M are also outlined.

There are more than 1,000 films, 2,000 photos, and 1,500 books in the museum. Every afternoon at 2 P.M. the museum shows an introductory film that runs about thirty minutes. A short video narrated by Keith Jackson is featured in a small theater.

EVEN WITH ALL THIS, the Bryant Museum is relatively small and can be covered in a short time. It is beautifully designed and laid out, and moves a visitor from one section to another quickly because of its superb organization.

The museum is not just for football buffs; it is for everyone, especially youngsters. Tour groups are encouraged. There is a small admission charge.

One of the most emotional experiences for me at the museum was a small video presentation called *Tribute to a Legend*. Some of the words, sung by John Chance Jones, are:

> Bear of Alabama
> Hero of little boys and their dads
> Thanks for all the memories and victories we shared
> We love you and miss you, Bear

The most indelible theme in the museum is Coach Bryant's character, from his humble upbringing in Arkansas, through his days playing for the Tide, when he played an important game against Tennessee with a broken bone in his leg, and later, as he climbed the head-coach ladder that ultimately led to international fame and, since his death, to a place of reverence in the hearts of millions.

In the museum is a replica of John David Crow's Heisman Trophy, a jersey worn by Steve Sloan, the football used in the Alabama-Auburn game that gave Coach Bryant his record-setting 315th victory, making him the winningest coach in American football history; along with a Bill Curry sweater and the "lucky tie" of Ray Perkins, and other items identified with the careers of Bart Starr, Joe Namath, Lee Roy Jordan, and other Bama football stars.

COACH BRYANT ARRIVED at the university in 1931 in the rumble seat of a Ford driven by assistant coach Hank Crisp, who had discovered the lanky, rangy teenager in Arkansas and brought him to Tuscaloosa to play football.

At the height of his years at the University, Bryant said, "I'm just a plow hand from Arkansas, but I've learned over the years how to lift some men up, how to calm down others, until finally they've got one heartbeat, together as a team."

Finally, on that cold winter day when it was all over, students and other people outside the church at his funeral stood with tears streaming down their faces. Perhaps the most poignant tribute of all came as the funeral procession moved slowly up Interstate 59 between Tuscaloosa and Birmingham, where Coach Bryant is buried. As the cortege rolled under the overpasses, schoolchildren stood on the railings above, holding up signs that read "Bear, We Love You."

For more information: Paul W. Bryant Museum hours are from 9 A.M. to 4 P.M. seven days a week. Closed major holidays. Admission $2 for adults and $1 for children. Phone or write Paul W. Bryant Museum, 300 Paul W. Bryant Drive, Box 870385, Tuscaloosa, AL 35487-0385. Phone (205) 348-4668.

Biltmore Estate

One Man's Dream, America's Treasure

THE YOUNG MAN was only twenty-three years old and was on holiday in the Blue Ridge Mountains of western North Carolina near Asheville. From the crest of the mountain range he looked down and saw a majestic and green valley with a curved river threading through it. Then and there he decided to build a house in that valley. He bore one of the greatest names in American history and, happily for future generations, he had the vision, determination, imagination—and above all the money—to fashion his house to his exact and vivid dreams.

The young man was George Washington Vanderbilt, grandson of the mighty American industrial titan Cornelius Vanderbilt. This was in the late 1880s. Grover Cleveland was president, the country was at peace, and capitalism was in full flower.

As young Mr. Vanderbilt visualized his house from the mountaintop, he saw a resplendent European mansion overlooking the tumbling mountain river and surrounded by the deep forests, virgin and green. Looking out over the valley he saw a vast estate patterned after the spacious French chateaux of the Loire Valley, but built with American ideas and ingenuity. Like its French counterparts, this estate would be a working farm. When construction began, Mr. Vanderbilt's estate totaled 125,000 acres and included Mount Pisgah.

The young man who stood on that mountainside and visualized the house and grounds that now form America's premier estate was no ordinary man. He was bookish—some would say intellectual—and well traveled, at home in other countries and other cultures. He was given more to philosophy than business, unlike his father and grandfather. He was also interested in agriculture.

Biltmore, with 250 rooms, is the largest residence in the U.S. Built by George Washington Vanderbilt and completed in 1895, the home is filled with antiques and art objects, and is surrounded by miles of landscaped grounds.

Photo courtesy of Biltmore Estate.

The entrance hall sets the tone of the great house. The sculpture portrays Roger carrying off Angelique on the Hippogriff.
Photo courtesy of Biltmore Estate.

THE HOUSE AND GROUNDS that George Washington Vanderbilt visualized from the mountainside have now become an American treasure, drawing thousands of visitors to Asheville every year.

I spent one of the most enchanting days of my life wandering around the estate. It is simply a marvel, perfectly preserved, a tribute to vision and the American way; an incomparable celebration of man's ingenuity and nature's wonders. With 250 rooms, Biltmore Estate is the largest private residence in America, and is a National Historic Landmark. I have never recommended a visit with more alacrity and high promise.

True to his vision and the family's tradition of quality and excellence, young Mr. Vanderbilt acquired the enthusiastic services and formidable talents of two fellow Americans who were absolutely at the top of their professional form: architect Richard Morris Hunt and landscape architect Frederick Law Olmsted.

Mr. Hunt's background included designing the base of the Statue of Liberty, several buildings at Harvard, Yale, and Princeton universities, palatial homes in New York and Newport, Rhode Island, and other landmark American structures.

Mr. Olmsted had essentially redefined landscape design in America. His credentials were dazzling: New York's Central Park, the Chicago World's Fair, the Stanford University campus, and more than two thousand parks. The fine hand of Olmsted is still evident throughout the grounds of the estate, a masterful touch that will live for centuries. (To underscore his importance, Olmsted has been featured in an hour-long PBS tribute.)

In the construction of the house and grounds, which Mr. Vanderbilt surely must have known would become a national treasure and landmark, nothing was spared, nothing overlooked, nothing overstated. The most modern technology was incorporated, including central heating, plumbing, elevators, refrigeration, and electrical systems. Some of Thomas Edison's new light bulbs were used. The walls were of Indian limestone. The estate was the wonder of those times, just as it is the wonder of these times.

The project took five years, and on Christmas Eve of 1895 George Vanderbilt opened his great house with a memorable party for his family and friends.

Vanderbilt died in 1914. In the true interest of public service, Mrs. Vanderbilt gave a large share of the grounds to form what is now Pisgah National Forest, which surrounds the estate.

The ceremonial banquet hall measures 72 x 42 feet and the ceiling arches rise 70 feet. The home is one of America's artistic and cultural treasures.

Photo courtesy of Biltmore Estate.

Fortunately the magnificent house and the remaining grounds, now called Biltmore Estate, were opened to the public for tours in 1930. Literally hundreds of thousands of Americans and international visitors have come to marvel at this distinctive masterpiece, which is an American manor home, yet a home with strong and indelible European overtones.

The house includes a collection of decorative art including paintings by Renoir and Pellegrini, portraits by Boldoni, Sargent, and Whistler, sixteenth-century Flemish tapestries, Meissen porcelains, and engravings by Albrecht Durer. Today the estate houses more than seventy thousand priceless art objects.

The restoration, remodeling, additions, and changing have been perpetual since the beginning. The Pellegrini ceiling in the library was completed in 1982; the Deerpark Restaurant, once a barn, was opened in 1979; three bedrooms were returned to their original decor in 1983; the stable was restored and opened as the Stable Cafe; and the Carriage House and Tack Rooms were opened in 1987. The Biltmore Estate Winery—a must-see—built in the restored dairy complex, was opened in 1985. Therefore the Biltmore Estate is now not only a fantastic worldwide attraction, but a living tribute to the memory of George Washington Vanderbilt.

BILTMORE ESTATE, in my opinion, is simply the most elegant house in America and perhaps the world.

The magnificence starts at Lodge Gate. The approach road winds for three miles of matchless landscape to Biltmore House. The long drive from the gate to the house reminded me of the driveway leading to Sutton Place, the English manor home of my friend, the late J. Paul Getty, and my visits there, and his magnificent art collection, which after his death was moved to the Getty Museum in California.

A visitor coming into the Biltmore grand entrance hall is first attracted to the center table where there is a set of bronzes by Antoine-Louis Barye. The center sculpture portrays Roger carrying off Angelique on a Hippogriff. The nearby candelabra are supported by the figures of Juno, Minerva, and Venus, and are crowned by the Three Graces. Such is the splendor of Biltmore House, evident in every hallway, every chamber, every room. Among the many items on the estate are a hanging that once belonged to Cardinal Richelieu and a gaming table once owned by Napoleon.

The vastness of the entire estate seems to cover not only acres but miles. From the house to the winery was at least three miles.

The first wine grapes were planted on Biltmore Estate in the early 1970s. Now the estate produces both red and white wines, and there are more than a hundred acres of grapes under cultivation. The winery is the most-visited in the U.S.; Biltmore wines are available at the estate, and in the states of North Carolina, South Carolina, Georgia, and Tennessee.

Biltmore Estate remains under the ownership of the Vanderbilt family. It is open to the public daily except Thanksgiving and Christmas. There is an admission charge, and a full day should be set aside for the visit. Lunch is available on the estate, or picnics are encouraged.

Biltmore Estate is located off Interstate 40 (exits 50 or 50B) near Asheville. For more information, contact Biltmore Estate, 1 North Pack Square, Asheville, NC 28801. Phone 1-800-543-2961 or 1-800-624-1575. Web site www.biltmore.com.

Historic Natchez
A Tradition of Beautiful Homes

T HE YEAR WAS 1932, and across this bountiful land most Americans were living a life of quiet desperation. It was in the days of the Great Depression. Stressful times were everywhere. In the Deep South, especially Mississippi, people were fighting a constant battle for economic survival. This was singularly true of a hamlet on the high bluffs above the Mississippi River. The town was Natchez, whose history, sometimes written in blood, was etched deep in the affairs of the nation.

The little city had enjoyed a golden era in the days of King Cotton. Written reports state that, prior to the outbreak of the Civil War, seventy-five millionaires lived in America and eleven of them lived in Natchez.

In those days, these men and their compatriots presided over a civilization with few equals in the way of opulent living. In keeping with their order, they built magnificent homes with wood from virgin forest, and filled them with splendid furniture, drapes, tapestries, rugs, silver, china, and paintings.

Some have said that this lifestyle was even grander than the fabled *Gone with the Wind* times in Georgia. After all, Natchez had the Mississippi River, with New Orleans only a short steamboat ride away, and Europe beyond. Too, the river always meant romance and sophistication, and Natchez was the oldest city on the Mississippi.

Its gracious people received the famous men of the day in their great homes: Henry Clay, Mark Twain, Aaron Burr, Andrew Jackson, and that gallant Frenchman, the toast of the new nation, Gen. Lafayette.

The good times rolled in Natchez for many years. Then subtly, as if moved by an unseen hand, things changed.

The reasons are many and perhaps not simple: the Civil War, the decline of cotton, and the coming of the railroads, which left the vaunted steamboats high and dry on the wharves of Natchez, New Orleans, Memphis, and St. Louis. It was almost like the visitor returning to Gatsby's great house from "the ends of the earth" after the tragedy, not realizing the "party was over."

Fortunately, the grand and glorious old homes still stand in Natchez. The high style and good judgment of Natchez gentry, handed down from generation to generation, precluded the destruction of these timeless structural masterpieces. True, the color had faded, some of the flair was gone, and many were in desperate need of paint and repair, but they were there: tangible, essential, august, white-pillared monuments to a resplendent past.

Many believe that in time of trouble, need, and vicissitude, it is the women who come forward and take charge, as in the Greek play *Lysistrata* by Aristophanes. Thus was born, in the darkness of the Great Depression, the internationally famous Natchez Pilgrimage.

Side view of the Briars. Note the many windows, typical of construction in that era.
Photo courtesy of Natchez Convention Center.

THE LADIES OF THE TOWN—intelligent, forward-thinking, steely eyed, determined, resourceful, perhaps omniscient—looked over their shapely shoulders at a gilded past and set about building a glorious future in the colorful Pilgrimage.

Built in 1860–61, Longwood is the largest octagonal house still in existence in America.

Photo by Starr Smith.

Today, throughout the year, thousands of visitors from the world over come to the old river town to tour the stately, regal, and awe-inspiring old mansions, and to marvel at the splendor of a bygone Southern way of life. While visitors are allowed to tour most of the homes at regularly scheduled times during the year, the full flavor of the city comes forth during the Spring Pilgrimage in March and the Fall Pilgrimage in October. Actual dates vary, so it's a good idea to check with the Natchez Convention and Visitors Bureau before making final plans. Phone toll-free 1-800-647-6724, or 601-446-6345.

I spent my high-school days in a Mississippi town called Magnolia, less than a hundred miles from Natchez, yet I had never been there until recently, when I had a guided tour of the marvelous old mansions. It is another world, a series of movie sets from a different age, a movable feast of antebellum splendor. These are not only memorable architectural wonders, but most have vast historical significance. For example, Jefferson Davis married Miss Varina Howell at the lovely home called the Briars, built in 1812.

The Briars, built in 1812, where future Confederate president Jefferson Davis married Miss Varina Howell on February 26, 1845.

In his book *Jefferson Davis: American Patriot*, Hudson Strode, my old friend and mentor at the University of Alabama, described the Briars this way:

> The house was on a 98-acre estate half a mile south of Natchez, and stood on a high bluff about 200 yards from the Mississippi. It was a story-and-a-half construction. A charming house, painted white, it sat high above the ground, with a wide veranda extending the length of the facade, and with four graceful dormer windows breaking the high slanting roof . . . The striking feature was the back drawing room, which ran the entire length of the house, with its back wall formed entirely of floor-to-ceiling windows.

Melrose, on eighty-four acres, a blend of Greek Revival and Georgian architecture built around 1845, contains Italian marble fireplaces, hand-carved Victorian furniture, and painted English floorcloths.

Then there are the Auburn (1812), D'evereux (1840), Dunleith (1856), Edgewood (1850), the Elms (1804), Landsdowne (1853, on the National Register of Historical Places), Linden (1800), Longwood (1860–61, the largest octagonal house remaining in America), Magnolia Hall (1858), Monmouth (1818), Rosalie (1820), Stanton Hall (1858), and scores of others, all breathtaking.

Some are available for bed and breakfast. Altogether there are more than five hundred antebellum homes and buildings in Natchez, most built between 1789 and 1860.

BUT THERE IS MORE to Natchez than colorful old homes.

It is now a vibrant and progressive little city with a sound economy and the friendliest people I've ever met. The Natchez Trace begins there and winds through America's most beautiful countryside, five hundred miles to Nashville, through Kosciusko, which is the birthplace of Oprah Winfrey, James Meredith, and a certain journalist who shall remain nameless.

Jefferson College is in Natchez, named for Thomas Jefferson and once attended by Jefferson Davis. Mickey Gilley was born in Natchez, and pepper jelly was first concocted there. Jim Bowie and Davy Crockett fought on the riverfront. The great steamboats *American Queen*, *Delta Queen*, and *Mississippi Queen* out of New Orleans make regular calls, bringing thousands of visitors year-round.

In downtown Natchez is the delightful remodeled old Eola Hotel, evoking memories of other times, and a far cry from the modern motels that surround the city: Comfort Inn, Isle of Capri, Prentiss Inn, Days Inn, Ramada Hilltop, Natchez Inn, Lady Luck Casino Hotel, and others.

When I last visited, we had a really first-class lunch at the King's Tavern on Jefferson Street, with a fine dry white wine of muscadine grapes produced at Natchez's Old South Winery. That night it was barbecue in Wharf Master's House at Natchez-Under-the-Hill, the riverfront area of restaurants, bars, night clubs and lounges, all arousing thoughts of bygone river days and nights.

Hollywood has not overlooked the movie possibilities of Natchez. Scores of films and television shows have been made there: *Huck Finn*, *The Autobiography of Miss Jane*

Pittman, the late Lonnie Coleman's *Beulah Land*, and Willie Morris's *Good Old Boy*, among others.

Natchez is naturally proud of its status as an international showcase. People come, leave, and tell their friends about it. Then they come again. Yet, lurking behind the glamorous tours and the glorious times personified by the great homes is American history of epic extent and significance.

The Indians from which the city gets its name were there first, and departed in the most tragic manner.

THE NATCHEZ INDIANS, a small tribe, were a quiet and peaceful lot who lived for generations along the Mississippi River, hunting buffalo and worshiping their gods.

Melrose, contructed in 1845 on eighty-four acres of giant oaks, magnolias, and flowering shrubs.

The first white man to see the bluffs that tower over the Mississippi River was the restless and legendary French explorer LaSalle, who came down the river around 1682 seeking the mouth of the great stream. He claimed the entire region in the name of France. He also saw the commanding potential of the bluffs, and a few years later the flag of France was raised over the newly established Fort Rosalie, which later became Natchez.

For a few years, the Natchez Indians and these legions of France lived in harmony. Then came tragedy. The Indians were angered because the French commander seized one of their sacred villages for his own use. They stormed the French garrison, killing many of the intruders. The French retaliated, wiping out the entire Natchez Indian nation.

Today on the site of the massacre stands the Grand Village of the Natchez Indians, a National Historical Landmark administered by the Mississippi Department of Archives and History.

But even before the massacre, the remaining days of French rule were numbered. At the close of the French and Indian War in 1764, the British moved into the area and hauled up the Union Jack. To encourage settlement, they immediately awarded large land grants. Then came the American Revolution, and King George III and his minions had their hands full along the Eastern seaboard. Because the English were occupied, Spaniards seized the opportunity to rule and moved quietly into the territory. They were even more generous in making land grants than the departed English. Once the American Revolution had been fought and won, Americans seeking opportunity in both the West and South came to Natchez. By 1798 the Spanish were gone.

In 1801 a treaty with the remaining Indian tribes signaled an event that, along with the later arrival of the steamboats, guaranteed the history and future prosperity of Natchez: the opening of the Natchez Trace, a walking trail used by riverboat men who took goods down the Mississippi River to New Orleans, and then rode or walked back to Nashville, Tennessee. This gave Natchez outlets by both land and water, and ushered in the fabulous reign of King Cotton. It was during this opulent period that many of the Natchez Pilgrimage homes were built and furnished.

There was a slight distraction in 1807 when Aaron Burr was arraigned for treason at an outdoor hearing under the giant campus oaks of Jefferson College, only a few miles from Natchez. A little farther away, at Woodville, Mississippi, a young man was growing up who was destined to become president of the Confederacy—Jefferson Davis. He was married in Natchez on February 26, 1845.

The gods of good fortune continued to smile on Natchez during the Civil War. Although Vicksburg was under siege not far to the north, only a few random shells from a Union gunboat fell on the bluffs near Natchez. At war's end the city hoped to return to the old order, but it was not to be. Natchez was stranded economically between the bygone days of the cotton kingdom and the oncoming rush of the "iron monster"—the railroads. It seemed that the glory days of the steamboats were gone forever.

But the City of Five Flags has survived and prospered, thanks to the lure of history, the determination of its ladies, the wisdom of its people, and the elegant and graceful antebellum mansions. And through the Pilgrimage, the majesty of Natchez lives on.

For more information, contact the Director, Convention and Visitors Commission, 640 Canal St., Natchez, MS 39120. Phone (601) 446-6345. The Natchez city web site is www.natchez.ms.us.

Alabama's Grand Hotel
Storied Treasure on Mobile Bay

ALABAMA'S FAMED Grand Hotel at Point Clear on Mobile Bay is now more than 150 years old. One would think that the great "Queen of Southern Resorts" would be resting on its laudable laurels. Far from it. Moving forward with spirited dispatch and an inspired long-range plan—ambitious new owners have taken over the reins of the Grand, and already a fortuitous trend is underway—that includes additional rooms and suites and a creative bayfront development program.

However, brisk and presumptuous innovation is not the order of the day at the Grand. Deep-rooted tradition and a watchful awareness of the status quo by a distinguished guest list have set the subtle, yet progressive, guidelines for the current entrepreneurs as they adroitly bring the Grand into the twenty-first century. It has been a delicate balance between preserving the unique, traditional, distinctive Southern ambience of the Grand of other days, and coupling it with modern hotel-operating techniques and advanced methods consistent with high-level resort management.

Happily, the point man on the scene, entrusted to protect the Grand's stylish ways and still preside over the upgrading of the venerable hotel to top resort standards, is general manager John Irvin. He has been at the Grand for quite a while and, being a Southern boy from Virginia, he understands things like tradition and style.

Mr. Irvin is one of the most dynamic, experienced, and forward-thinking young hotel men in America. Moreover he is diplomatic. He has juggled the competing interests well, to the applause of the year-by-year crowd and the younger and new aficionados, as well as buoyant and elated convention guests.

Today's Grand Hotel, carrying on a splendid 150-year-old tradition, remains the Queen of Southern Resorts.

Mr. Irvin says, "What we are trying to do here at the Grand is maintain the style and grace of other days, and yet at the same time give the best possible service and luxurious appointments to our guests. People who come to the Grand have a very high degree of expectations. We must fulfill their every wish and desire. Our guest-to-staff ratio is one-to-one, and our employees are a vital part of the Grand's popularity. So what we have here is a really fine old hotel, luxurious and stylish standards, a perfect location, balmy weather, and seasoned staff members who love their jobs and like to serve the guests of the Grand."

THE GRAND IS SET on a 550-acre parklike peninsula that stretches out into Mobile Bay, surrounded by subtropical foliage, ancient magnolias, and moss-draped oaks, some more than a hundred years old. Nearby are the picturesque homes of longtime eastern-shore residents.

Across Highway 98 is the Grand's highly acclaimed 36-hole Lakewood golf course, which has challenged the skill of Sam Snead, Byron Nelson, and a host of younger players on the PGA tour. Lakewood is now a featured course on Alabama's fabled Robert Trent Jones Golf Trail.

Activities available at the Grand include sailing, fishing, horseback riding, and bicycling. The new swimming pool complex features waterfalls and slides for the kids and an adult pool with whirlpools. The pool area is near Mobile Bay and the newly refurbished Grand beach.

When completed early in 2002, the new rooms and suites will overlook the Bay, the marina, and the gardens of the Grand. This building will also include a spa, health club, and indoor swimming pool. When additions are complete, the Grand will have a total of four hundred rooms and suites.

In my many years of going to the Grand, I have found that young people are coming more and more, and they are bringing their children. Yet the old traditions live on. At the Grand it is traditional to dress for dinner. Most gentlemen wear jackets in the Grand Dining Room and in the elegant Bayview Restaurant, fronting on the Bay, in the evening. High tea is served in the lobby every afternoon at 4 P.M.

Chester Hunt, at the Grand since 1941, is the hotel's historian. He gives enlightening lecture tours for guests.

Photo by Starr Smith.

Over the years the Grand has evolved into a major convention hotel while maintaining its personal and distinctive appeal for guests who are seeking the ultimate in resort vacation life. However, when a convention is being held at the Grand, the hotel likes a fifty-fifty mix between delegates and vacationing guests.

Rare, novel, and unusual services or gestures are offered by the hotel. Fresh complimentary herbs are from the chef's own herb garden. Bartenders in the celebrated Bird Cage Lounge decorate a mint julep with mint from the Grand's private patch. The kitchen will cook a guest's fish dinner, after he or she has caught the fish off the Grand pier.

Among the many truly appealing things about the Grand are the employees, called associates, some of whom are third generation. Bucky Miller, who for decades presided as the beaming chief bartender in the Bird Cage Lounge, has been at the Grand for sixty years. He is now the Grand's Ambassador, greeting guests in the lobby and dining rooms. Chester Hunt, at the Grand since 1941, is the Grand's historian, and gives highly personal and enlightening lecture tours for guests. Alfred Agee, head bellman, proudly wears a fifty-year Grand Hotel pin.

There is a remarkable fusion, a feeling of camaraderie, unity, and fellowship among new and old Grand associates. Many are college trained and, under general manager Irvin's guidance and professional tutelage, will climb the ladder in the hospitality business. The Grand is a happy hotel with outgoing, super-friendly people, and the guests are well aware of this.

SEEING THE GRAND Hotel for the first time in its lush setting on Mobile Bay at Point Clear, a visitor would never think that the great old institution is one of the world's most

durable survivors. But it is. The Grand has lived through three fires, six major wars, the Great Depression, numerous hurricanes—two of them deadly—and now is moving with grace and style into the twenty-first century. The Grand has also entertained a star-spangled guest list—a president, senators, generals, diplomats, foreign leaders, sports figures, and entertainment stars. The Glenn Miller Orchestra plays often at the Grand.

Having spent a considerable and joyful part of my life in and out of the Grand, I once wrote a story equating it with two other traditional American

Bucky Miller, former chief bartender in the Bird Cage Lounge, has been at the Grand for sixty years. He now greets guests as the hotel's Ambassador.

Photo by Starr Smith.

Fan Joe

She comes down to the Grand early in December every year from her home in Mississippi—a charming lady known simply as Fan Joe. She's been coming to the Grand every year at Christmas time for thirty-five years. Fan Joe is Mrs. Louis Fleischer of Greenville, a town on the Mississippi River. For many years she came with her husband, Louis. After he died in 1986 she continued to come, staying in the same room they had occupied year after year.

After a month or six weeks, Manager John Irvin sends her back home to Mississippi in the Grand's limousine. Her driver is the mannered and courtly Chester Hunt, who has been at the Grand as long as Fan Joe as been coming there. On the morning of her departure, the hotel's chef fixes a box lunch, the Cadillac is pulled up to the curved driveway, and the staff comes out in force to see her off. Mr. Irvin gives her a farewell kiss, Mr. Hunt tucks a blanket around her in the back seat, everybody waves, and, in a style not unlike a certain movie, "Miss Daisy" is on her way home. Mr. Irvin says, "We always give a lot of attention to our guests who have been coming for a long time, but I must admit, Fan Joe is like family. She has the same table at every meal. Everybody in the dining room wants to wait on her, but they take turns. She has a smile and a good word for all of them." Mr. Irvin and his wife, Nancy, always have dinner with Fan Joe on New Year's Eve.

I first met Fan Joe at a Christmas Eve party around the magnificent fireplace in the lobby. Looking across the crowded room, I saw a lovely lady with a glowing smile and sparkling eyes. I decided that I had to meet this luminous person, so I went over, introduced myself, and we have been friends ever since.

Fan Joe was born and grew up in Greenville, Mississippi, and attended Northwestern University in Chicago. When she married Louis Fleischer, they went to live in Shaw, Mississippi, near Greenville, and ran a general store for many years. After Louis's death, Fan Joe returned to Greenville.

Fan Joe has many friends all over America. One of her oldest buddies is Shelby Foote, the Civil War historian and lecturer. They were in high school together and have remained friends over the years. Another old friend was the late Hodding Carter, publisher-editor of the Greenville *Delta Times-Democrat* and a Pulitzer prize winner, and his wife, Betty. She watched their son grow up—Hodding Carter III, the Washington columnist and television commentator—and she takes great pride in his national reputation. She is also a friend of Bern Keating, the famous writer, and his wife, Frankie, the renowned photographer, who live in Greenville.

One winter afternoon, over a dry sherry in the Bird Cage Lounge as we watched the rippling whitecaps in the bay, I talked to Fan Joe about friends and friendships. With a smile and a slight tip of her wine glass, she paraphrased Samuel Johnson, "If we don't make new friends as we move along through life, we will soon find ourselves left alone. I try to keep my friendships in good repair." One place Fan Joe does that is at the Grand Hotel.

Fan Joe (Mrs. Louis Fleischer of Greenville, Mississippi, on left) visits the hotel every year at Christmas. Here she enjoys a chat with John Irvin, the hotel's general manager, and his wife, Nancy.

Photo by Starr Smith.

resorts, the Homestead and the Greenbrier. I've changed my mind. While all three are venerable, luxurious, and time-honored, only the Grand has experienced life in this world to the fullest, not only surviving, but prevailing. The Grand is simply in a class unto itself, a fabulous Southern monument, not only to a glorious past but also to a matchless future. John Irvin and the Alabama-oriented owners seem to be dedicated to this end with a meticulous and exacting game plan.

A bit of Grand history: In the sixteenth century a roving Spanish admiral, Alonso Alvarez de Pineda, came in from the sea to discover a lovely finger of land jutting out into Mobile Bay. This was Point Clear. Like many of his countrymen, this Spanish sailor was a man of superb taste. He quickly recognized beauty and quality. Perhaps the admiral himself surmised that, two centuries later, there would rise on those grounds a magnificent hotel.

Life for the hotel began in 1847. It had forty rooms in several buildings on the peninsula. During the Civil War a Union gunboat fired on the hotel, which was used as a Confederate garrison and field hospital. One of the buildings was severely damaged and was later rebuilt. At the hotel/hospital were Southern fighting men who had been wounded in the Battle of Vicksburg. Today 150 unidentified Confederate soldiers are buried at a site near the Grand's Lakewood golf course.

In 1869 and again in 1871 fires all but destroyed the hotel.

IN 1875 CAPT. H. C. Baldwin started anew. He built a new hotel and for the first time called it the Grand. The hotel was sold again in 1890 to James E. Glennon, who operated it for many years. Those were the glory days for the Grand. The gentry came on holiday from far and wide—New Orleans, Atlanta, Pensacola, Montgomery, Memphis, Jackson, the new city of Birmingham, and other points. The Grand became a glamorous meeting place for well-bred gentle folk of an emerging and highly social South. One might say those beautiful people were the jet-setters of their day.

That's the way it was for those first few decades of the twentieth century—tradition, luxury, ambience, peer appeal—a wonderful resort in a perfect setting, catering to the elite of the South. And they returned year after year, generation after generation.

The Grand was sold in 1939, this time to an imaginative Mobile entrepreneur named Ed Roberts. Even with the war clouds gathering in Europe, Mr. Roberts saw the immense possibilities of the Grand. He demolished the main building and in 1941 built the present central building, which is still the center point for the complex.

In World War II the Grand was used for military training, and even now the commandant of those days returns every year, requesting the room that he used as an office during the war.

Other owners were involved in the years following the war: the Waterman Steamship Co. of Mobile, Southern Industries, and the McLean interests.

In 1979 came an almost fatal blow to the Grand. Hurricane Frederick virtually destroyed the property and brought on an almost insuperable financial problem.

Enter now, in 1981, the Marriott corporation, one of America's premier hotel resort owners and operators. They immediately set about building a new conference center, constructing 176 new rooms for a total of 307, and adding 9 holes to the Lakewood golf course. The Marriott people succeeded in forging a sound and ongoing combination of high-level conventions, the old Grand clientele, and young guests seeking a luxurious resort with high standards and old traditions. After Marriott, there were several changes of ownership. Now, fortunately, the Grand is owned by Point Clear Holdings, Inc., headed by Edward J. Kulik, with Alabama investors involved—assuring a strong and stable entry into the twenty-first century.

So the Grand goes on, year by year, offering those subtle and special things: tradition, ambience, personal service, the surprise gesture, and, above all, luxurious accommodations and superb food. These are the Grand features that bring guests back, generation after generation.

Contact the Grand Hotel, One Grand Blvd., Point Clear, AL 36564-0639. Phone (334) 928-9201, reservations (800) 544-9933. Web site www.marriottgrand.com.

Silver Springs

Where Glass-Bottom Boats Ply the Eternal Waters

OCALA, FLORIDA, is where Marjorie Kinnan Rawlings wrote her Pulitzer Prize–winning book, *The Yearling*, and where the great racehorse Affirmed was born, eventually winning the Kentucky Derby, Preakness, and Belmont, striding into history as the last winner of the vaunted Triple Crown. The Tarzan movies, starring Olympic swimmer Johnny Weissmuller, were made here, and Lloyd Bridges filmed his popular television series *Sea Hunt* nearby. The weather is always temperate in the low rolling hills, dotted with live oak trees that measure their age in centuries. The Indians were here first, and later came the Spanish conquistadors. Now the land is one of America's most dazzling tourist attractions, drawing more than a million people every year.

This is star country in central Florida's storied Marion County. But the real and abiding star of Ocala is not a book, a horse, or a Hollywood movie. It's a natural phenomenon called Silver Springs—the world's mightiest artesian stream. Perhaps, in a manner of speaking, everything that Ocala is today comes from the millions of gallons of water that gush from the Springs in an endless flow. The strong outpouring of water has been going on for 10,000 years, and for more than 150 years Silver Springs has been beguiling visitors as one of nature's most appealing attractions, and as Florida's original tourist mecca.

The overflowing magic of nature, and the underwater kingdoms of Silver Springs, have put Ocala on the tourist maps of the world. But Marion County has more than enough entertainment magic to keep visitors, especially families, occupied for days on end. The alluring list of entertainment possibilities seems to go on and on—Ocala National Forest, Juniper Springs, National Recreation Trail, the Historic District with 207 history-laden buildings, the nationally acclaimed Appleton Museum of Art, antique shops, world-

Main entrance to one of Florida's most famous attractions.
Photo by Starr Smith.

Amazing animals in every way, turtles are a longtime attraction at Silver Springs.
Photo by Starr Smith.

class horse farms, Young's Paso Fino Ranch, a museum of drag racing, and other appealing venues for the discerning visitor.

YET WITH ALL THE appealing attractions of Marion County, the focal point and compelling magnet for a visitor remains the wondrous Silver Springs. This is an immovable feast in a magnificent setting. Still, it is always changing—new features are added, the old attractions seem to burnish with a refreshing glow, and Silver Springs tempts the visitor, young and old, with stellar enjoyment and Ocala's charm and sunshine.

The crystal-clear 99.7 percent pure spring water that forms the Silver River has been flowing for countless centuries, and clues have been found that human activity existed at Silver Springs in those long-ago times. It has been documented that Timucuan and Seminole Indian tribes settled at the Springs, and in the year 1598 Hernando de Soto led an expedition to the settlement then called Ocali. The Spanish explorers did not tarry long in the area, moving on in their quest for gold. But the Indians left behind a colorful history, and, in honor of their achievements, the glass-bottom boats at Silver Springs are named for great Seminole Indian chiefs.

These famous boats, which permit visitors to visually explore the arcane wonders of the Springs, were invented in 1878 at Silver Springs by a man named Hullam Jones. The glass-bottom boats have been constantly updated since that time, in keeping with the Silver Springs policy and desire to provide guests with the most modern and up-to-date techniques for viewing this outstanding facility.

So what started decades ago as a simple natural attraction has now grown into one of America's prime vacation destinations. Today there is much more to Silver Springs than just the largest artesian spring formation in the world. True, that is the major attraction, but Silver Springs is now a 350-acre multitheme nature park that surrounds the headwaters of the Silver River.

Silver Springs has had a remarkably successful captive-breeding program. Twenty-two giraffes have been born at the park, and almost a hundred other species born or hatched.

Photo by Starr Smith.

Tourists on a glass-bottom boat lean over to see the underwater creations of nature. Glass-bottom boats were invented at Silver Springs.

Photo by Starr Smith.

Perhaps the entertainment evolution of Silver Springs began in the 1930s when Ross Allen, a legendary herpetologist, promoter, and showman, founded the Silver Springs Reptile Institute. Since then, reptiles have been synonymous with Silver Springs. Today a major feature of the park is the Reptiles of the World show, where animal handlers exhibit and explain the difference between snakes, alligators, crocodiles, and lizards. This is a fast-moving, entertaining twenty-minute show. The largest freshwater turtle in North America, tipping the scales at 110 pounds, is the star. Ross Allen brought the turtle to Silver Springs in 1937.

A VOYAGE ON THE Silver River on the glass-bottom boats is the highlight of a Silver Springs visit. Passengers have an unparalleled view of underwater life in the crystal-clear water. Boat captains, certified by the Coast Guard, provide an entertaining narration along the way, pointing out seven major spring formations and other points of interest as the boats slowly move over the water. Other major highlights of a visit include:

> Jeep Safari—zebra-striped jeeps carry visitors through thirty-five acres of specially designed animal habitats, where twenty species of free-roaming wildlife live casually and

free, including African waterbuck, four species of deer, Brazilian tapirs, sloths, and alligators in their own three-foot-deep pond.

Creature Feature—an exhibit of giant spiders, scorpions, hissing cockroaches, and a twenty-pound marine toad, all reminiscent of a late-night horror movie. Children love it.

Jungle Cruise—an exotic safari down the Fort King Waterway past twenty-two species of animals from six continents, including giraffes, zebras, emus, and ostriches.

Amazing Pets—domestic dogs and cats from local humane shelters have been taught to perform unusual tricks.

Doolittle's Petting Zoo—brings visitors close to baby animals, including sheep, llama, antelope, deer, and a giraffe.

Lost River Voyage—visitors cruise down the Silver River to an untouched and untamed version of the Florida of long ago—ancient cypress trees line the banks of the river and alligators, ospreys, giant gar fish, and blue herons live as they did thousands of years ago. In total, 29 varieties of water birds, 109 different kinds of water plants, 11 kinds of turtles, and 36 species of fish inhabit the Silver River.

Silver Springs has more than a hundred species of exotic wildlife on display from around the world. The park has had a remarkable and successful captive-breeding program, including Khama and Khimba, two giraffes born several years ago, and now the proud parents of a six-foot-tall young male giraffe. Altogether, twenty-two giraffes have been born at the park and almost a hundred other species have been either born or hatched.

Over the years I have visited Silver Springs many times—every visit a new adventure. I never tire of viewing the wonders of the waters from the glass-bottom boats. My recommendation: Plan to spend a full day at the park, located at 5656 East Silver Springs Boulevard, Silver Springs, FL 34488, one mile east of Ocala and ten miles east of Interstate 75. There are more than a hundred hotels and motels in the area, and several bed and breakfast inns. Silver Springs is open from 9 A.M. to 5:30 P.M., and longer in the summertime and holidays. Parking is free and the park provides a shaded kennel service. A variety of food is available at the Springside Pizzeria, Outback Restaurant, Billy Bowlegs Restaurant, and the Fudge Show.

For more information, contact Silver Springs, P.O. Box 370, Silver Springs, FL 34489-0370. Phone (800) 234-7458 or (904) 236-2121. Web site www.silversprings.com.

Here are three nearby attractions worth checking out.

• Ocala is International Horse Country, one of four breeding and training centers in the world for thoroughbred racing horses. The others are Newcastle, England; Chantilly, France; and Lexington, Kentucky. In addition to Triple Crown winner Affirmed, Ocala has produced Needles, winner of the Kentucky Derby and Belmont; Carry Back, winner of the Kentucky Derby and Preakness; and Dr. Fager, Honest Pleasure, and other winners. Some horse farms allow visitors. Check with the Ocala/Marion County Chamber of Commerce at 110 Silver Springs Boulevard, Ocala FL 34470. Phone (352) 629-8051. Fax (352) 629-7651. Web site www.ocalacc.com.

• The world-class Appleton Museum of Fine Art is located at 4333 NE Silver Springs Boulevard in Ocala. This is an imposing marble building, set majestically on forty-four wooded acres, that houses more than six thousand works collected worldwide by founder Arthur Appleton. Phone (352) 236-1700.
    Web site www.fsu.edu/%7Esvad/Appleton/AppletonMuseum.html.

• The Don Garlits Museum of Drag Racing is a far cry from the Appleton, but still a major tourist attraction. The museum is the home of many famous race cars, along with a number of antique and restored cars. A highlight is the first car to exceed 250 miles per hour for the quarter-mile. For information: 13700 SW 16th Avenue, Ocala, FL 34473. Phone (352) 245-8661. Web site http://gnv.fdt.net/~garlits.

Colonial Williamsburg
In the South's Most Historic State

I T MAY SEEM STRANGE to have the name of John D. Rockefeller, Jr., mentioned in the same breath with George Washington, Thomas Jefferson, Patrick Henry, George Mason, and other great leaders and patriots of early America. Yet there is a strong, indelible, and magical link between the billionaire oil baron of modern times and the wise and hearty men of Colonial days who created our new and vibrant country more than 225 years ago. That link is Williamsburg, Virginia.

In those stirring days of Washington and Jefferson, Williamsburg was the citadel of American dreams. Echoing down the stately streets, and beyond to the vast stretches of the new land, were rich and resonant calls for freedom and independence. Williamsburg was the thriving capital of Virginia, which was, in that era, a powerful colony that stretched west to the Mississippi River and north to the Great Lakes. From 1699 to 1780 it was the largest and perhaps the most influential of the American colonies.

Not only was Williamsburg a sterling social and cultural center, but it was here that the basic concepts of the new republic were forged—individual liberty, self-government, responsible leadership, and a sense of public duty—by Washington, Jefferson, and their eager and rebellion-minded colleagues. It was in this small city that these strong and dedicated men, looking centuries ahead and dreaming no little dreams, reached political maturity, nurturing the ideas and ideals that led the American colonies to declare their independence and form a daring new nation unlike any other.

Because Williamsburg was one of the most important ideological spawning points for the leaders of the American independence movement, it is not too much to think that

The Capitol, seat of government when the Virginia colony stretched from the Atlantic Ocean to the Great Lakes and the Mississippi River. Site of Patrick Henry's famous "Caesar-Brutus" speech.

Printing office, post office, and bookbindery served as a communications hub in colonial times.
Photo courtesy of Colonial Williamsburg Foundation.

it, perhaps more than any other town, was the birthplace of the new country. True, it ranked as a cultural and political center along with New York, Boston, Philadelphia, and Charleston, but there is ample evidence to suggest that this little Tidewater city offered a bit more, perhaps ethereal. This something more is called dreams. After all, Williamsburg was the scene of defiant speeches against King George III, Patrick Henry's "Caesar-Brutus" speech, George Mason's Virginia Declaration of Rights, the introduction of Jefferson's Statute for Religious Freedom, and, on May 15, 1776, the Resolution for Independence, which led directly to the Declaration of Independence in Philadelphia on July 4 of that year.

Being an admirer of Thomas Jefferson, I was happy to find his charismatic presence everywhere in Williamsburg. He originally came there to attend the College of William and Mary, and made his first contacts with Washington, Patrick Henry, Randolph, and others in the movement for independence. And he was the last governor to live in the Palace before the capital city was moved.

RICHMOND BECAME the new capital. The Williamsburg rhythm changed then, and for generations the little city lived a quiet life of memories. Enter, in 1926, the towering and super-affluent presence of John D. Rockefeller, Jr., who not only had built a vast fortune, but, inspired by the vision of the Reverend W. A. R. Goodwin, then rector of the Bruton Parish Church, set about to restore Williamsburg to its pre-Revolutionary status and appearance. This was a wise choice because, as a practical matter, it was the only Colonial capital that would lend itself to restoration and a return to its greatest glory.

Mr. Rockefeller and his wife, Abby Aldrich, lived in Williamsburg and gave the project their personal leadership and untold financial support, and set a standard of excellence that still guides Colonial Williamsburg today. Mr. Rockefeller died in 1960, and even through his legacy includes heirs who rose to lofty positions in America's financial, cultural, social, and political worlds, there can be little doubt that Colonial Williamsburg is his greatest gift to his country. His fortune and uncompromising guidance contributed to the preservation of eighty-eight original structures and the reconstruction of fifty major buildings and many smaller ones, on their original sites.

Two-horsepower time machine carries tourists down Duke of Gloucester Street, the main road in Williamsburg in the eighteenth century.

Governor's Palace was the symbol of British power in colonial Virginia. It later served as headquarters for Thomas Jefferson and Patrick Henry.

After more than seventy-five years of preservation, restoration, and reconstruction, Colonial Williamsburg stands today as it did in the eighteenth century, recalling those years when it served as a seat of government in the uneasy times when determined leaders laid the foundation of the new republic. Simply stated, Colonial Williamsburg is a forceful, emotional, and thrilling reminder of the birth of this magnificent country, as well as a major source of its democratic principles. I believe it is the single most cogent, vivid, and graphic place in America to recall the memory of the people and events that made it all possible, because, really, it's where it all started.

I HAVE NEVER VISITED Williamsburg without a surging feeling of pride and thanks. Every man, woman, and child in America should visit the place. Actually, more than one million visitors come every year, from all fifty states and every continent. American presidents from Roosevelt through Clinton have come, some more than once, and more than a hundred heads of state have toured the historical site. If Disney World is for entertainment, then Williamsburg is about history and life in the early days of this country.

Yet Williamsburg is so well organized and professionally staged, and the place itself is so beautiful, that the historical story follows as a matter of easy course. It is magnificent and, to paraphrase Edward R. Murrow, Williamsburg is a monumental testament that we in America are not descendants of timid people. On my visits to St. Petersburg, Russia, I have marveled at the vast restoration wonders of Peter the Great's summer palace at Peterhof. Williamsburg is far, far more extensive, and, opulence aside, much more impressive.

It is one of the largest and most diversified museums in the world. Yet, buildings, gardens, and other physical reminders of the past cannot convey fully the meaning and significance of Williamsburg. Here is also living history—the active practice, by real living people, of numerous colonial-era crafts and trades ranging from blacksmiths to wigmakers. The knowing and skillful interpretive staff handles the exhibitions and presentations, and visitors are never at a loss to know what Williamsburg is all about. Nearly four thousand men and women work at Colonial Williamsburg, pointing up once again the scope of the entire operation.

The plan of 1699 is still used in the mile-long Duke of Gloucester Street, with the Wren Building of the College of William and Mary at one end and the Capitol at the other. Other buildings include the Governor's Palace, Printing Office, Post Office, Bookbindery, Courthouse, Wetherburn's Tavern, and Bruton Church—and of special interest, Basset Hall, the Williamsburg home of Mr. and Mrs. Rockefeller.

The starting point for any tour is the Visitors' Center. Information on programs, lodging, dining, and special events is available. Parking lots at the Center can handle up to two thousand cars, and shuttle buses run throughout the Historical Area at regular intervals. There is an admission charge. My suggestion is to start, at the very beginning, by seeing the orientation film *Williamsburg—The Story of a Patriot*. This thirty-five-minute film is extremely well done and sets the mood.

There are more than nine thousand hotel and motel rooms in the area, so visitors seldom have problems finding accommodations. To do full justice to Williamsburg, I suggest a two or three day visit. And, of course, it's the perfect place for kids.

For more information: Colonial Williamsburg is midway between Richmond and Norfolk on I-64 (exit 238). Mailing address is P.O. Box B, Williamsburg, VA, 23187. Phone 1-800-HISTORY. Web site is www.history.org.

Travels with Father
A Personal Memoir

LOOKING BACK NOW, I think my love for travel, and my first encounter with the outside world, came from my father. He died on a February day in 1987. Almost from the beginning of my life, he took me on road trips from the little Mississippi towns where we lived: Kosciusko, Starkville, Yazoo City, Magnolia. It was first to Jackson, then Greenville, Vicksburg, Biloxi, Gulfport, Mobile, and later to Memphis, Nashville, and Atlanta.

When I was about twelve, he took me to New Orleans, my first trip to that incomparable city, which, over my many years as a journalist, and travels to 103 different countries, has remained my favorite in all the world.

He was always ready for a trip—excited, curious about everything, an easy and reliable traveling companion. In those days when I traveled with him, he planned the trips and made the arrangements. He was a fine and careful planner, always open for side visits and interesting places and people.

In later years, I was able, in small measure, to return the favor by taking him on trips. Perhaps the most memorable of all was a long motor journey we made across the very face of America to California: the Grand Canyon, Las Vegas, Boulder Dam, Lake Tahoe, San Francisco, and the Pacific route to Los Angeles, Mexico, and Arizona. He followed the space program with avid interest and was like a schoolboy when I took him to Cape Canaveral in Florida. He was a country music lover and sat on the front row of the Ryman Auditorium when we went to Nashville for the Grand Ole Opry. On a tour of the White House he had the chance to tell President Dwight D. Eisenhower about his three sons and their service in World War II, one of them under the then general's direct command.

Strangely, Father had little interest in traveling overseas. We talked at times about a visit to England, Scotland, and especially Ireland, where his forefathers had lived. But he loved America so much that he never left this country except for a short side trip to Mexico. During World War II he kept pins on his world map showing the overseas locations of his sons, and always in my travels had a pin for the countries I visited.

After my Father died and summer came on, I wrote a story in his memory. This is that story:

THE SON HAS ALWAYS seen himself as a rather worldly man, perhaps even sophisticated in a low-key way.

He believes in the given order of things, the inevitability of life, and the ultimate design of destiny. A fatalist, he believes there is a time to live and a time to die. Therefore, one day years ago, as the Father's Day holiday approached, he was somewhat surprised to find his thoughts turning more and more to that February day a few months earlier, when his Father had been laid to final rest in a small green plot beneath giant oaks, near the country home where both Father and Son had passed perhaps the happiest time of their lives.

For more than half a century, the Father had been one of the vital and motivating forces in the life of the Son, and now, as Sunday approached, the Son realized that it would be the first Father's Day of his life without a father. Small wonder, then, that tender and poignant thoughts of a remarkable Father who had left such a legacy of love and hope flooded the memories of a grateful Son.

The Father was not a very impressive man in stature. He was a little short of six feet and well built. But it was his vivid personality, enormous energy, expressive face, sparkling eyes, and positive, exciting, eager attitude toward life that cast him in his own unforgettable mold. He talked to strangers in airports and always left with an invitation to come and see them in Houston, Memphis, or Albany, Georgia, or wherever. He was a favorite with the ladies and married extremely well. For the most part, he was a self-made

Father and Sons—(left to right) Air Force colonel Jim, Father, Starr, and Jay, a radio station owner. The Father was especially proud that all three sons served in the Air Force in World War II; he stuck pins in a world map to keep track of their location. Photo taken about 1970.

man, worked very hard, and combined a career in private industry with U.S. government service in the last years of his life.

Through it all, the Father was a serious man with a keen and appealing sense of humor. He was a gentle man, a Christian, and an American patriot. His greatest pride was his family: a lovely, enduring, and understanding wife, three sons, and two daughters. He was especially proud that his boys served their country in World War II.

On Father's Day, the Son was thinking of the Father not in philosophical terms and mundane accomplishments, but in gentle and human ways, those down-to-earth characteristics that go to make up a life.

He remembered in the 1930s, when the Father was an industry executive and, during a labor dispute, was forced to shoot one of the strikers in self-defense. The man didn't die but, until feelings about the shooting settled down, the Father spent a few days in out-of-town "protective custody." When the Son visited his Father in his confinement, which was in fact a jail, he found him playing his mandolin, advising the inmates on their problems, and discussing general philosophy. In less than a week, the Father was released with no charges filed. On his last night in jail, his fellow inmates gave a supper in his honor, with the guards bringing in special food.

The Father was not only a mandolin and violin player, he was also a baseball player of some note. The Son remembered the time his Father's company baseball team was playing a crucial game. The Father was sent in to pinch hit. He laced a single to right, stretched it into a double, and broke his foot sliding into second base. His hit won the game, but he spent weeks in a cast and on crutches, and could only grin sheepishly at the constant kidding of his three ball-playing sons. He was then about thirty-five.

IN THE POKER GAME of life, the Father was not dealt many face cards: little education, sketchy background, the Great Depression. But he patiently and shrewdly parlayed his small cards into straights, flushes, occasionally a full house, and more than once came up with a straight flush. Like the late Paul "Bear" Bryant, former President Harry Truman, and others of those Depression times, he learned early that his own hard work would have to be the key to his success, and perhaps even to his survival. But he was not disadvantaged. He had a natural proclivity for work and planning, a great outgoing personality, a positive attitude, eternal charm, and a deep and abiding faith in America.

The Father died at the age of ninety. The Son remembered the clear, bright, crisp, and sunny February day of his funeral. The gathering was small; the Father had outlived his friends and contemporaries. One of the pallbearers was a tall and distinguished-looking black man, Ellis Varnado, who had been reared by the Father along with his own sons. A granddaughter, a graduate of the Louisiana State University music department, sang "The Old Rugged Cross" and the preacher said a few words. At the cemetery the Father's beloved Masons conducted the age-old and impressive Scottish burial rites, and the Son watched his Mother lay a single red rose on the casket.

The Son thought then of the dramatic radio broadcast by his friend and colleague Edward R. Murrow, describing the courage of the English people during the bombing of London in World War II. It was Mr. Murrow's final tribute to the British people after the war was over, just before he returned to America. He ended the broadcast by saying, "You have lived a life, not an apology."

As he walked away from the grave on that February day, the Son thought how much that trenchant phrase, in full measure, described his Father—he had, indeed, lived a life, not an apology.

Having recently published a book in which his Father played a significant role, the Son was frequently asked to talk about his Father. He said, "He was not only a Father, he was a friend. He was not only lovable, he was likable. He lived in the most momentous times his country has ever known and loved every minute of it. He lived as a gentleman. He died with dignity, and we buried him on Valentine's Day."

The National Museum of Naval Aviation
From the Navy's First Plane to the Blue Angels

IT WAS CALLED *CORONADO*, and even the name seemed to carry overtones of excitement, legend, and greatness. It is a giant four-engine flying boat with two oval fins and a wingspan of 115 feet. Officially designated the PB2Y, the *Coronado* cruised at 150 miles per hour and had a range of 1,500 miles. In the last days of World War II, it was the personal airplane of Admiral Chester Nimitz, the navy's top commander in the Pacific. On September 2, 1945, it carried Nimitz and his staff to the formal surrender ceremonies in Tokyo Bay aboard the battleship USS *Missouri*. Today the *Coronado* is in a place of honor in the National Museum of Naval Aviation at the "Cradle of Naval Aviation," the historic naval air station in Pensacola, Florida.

The great *Coronado* is in distinguished company at the museum, which houses the most important collection of naval aircraft to be found anywhere. There are 182 full-scale authentic aircraft displayed either inside the museum or on its flight line outside. There are more than 290,000 square feet of exhibition space for the aircraft, space vehicles, memorabilia, models, art and photographs, cockpit trainers, and simulators. There are even two theaters. Especially appealing to kids is a hands-on educational area and a re-created aircraft ready-room.

The appealing way in which the museum is designed makes it easy for kids to explore on their own. It features a $4\frac{1}{2}$–story aircraft carrier island and flight deck modeled after the light carrier USS *Cabot*. Much of the carrier exhibit, including the 40mm guns, is "hands-on." The Flight Adventure Deck is also full of hands-on and aviation-oriented activities designed especially for kids. Believe me, it is all a kid's dream.

World War II jeep, used by Marines in island-hopping battles in the Pacific theater.

Still in formation, real planes once flown by the Blue Angels hang inside the museum.

Photos by Starr Smith.

Consisting of thirty-eight interactive displays that range from very simple to very sophisticated flight simulators, the Flight Adventure Deck represents a cooperative effort between the museum and local school districts to provide middle-school pupils an exciting "lab" that explores the atmosphere, gravity, mass and motion, and aerodynamics and propulsion. Complete with a curriculum, lesson plans, and two teachers on sabbatical to the museum, the program's goal is to inspire greater interest in math and science. When not used by school groups, the display is open to the public.

A LARGE NUMBER OF the aircraft on display at the museum are rare and one-of-a-kind. The star of the museum is probably the four-motored Curtis NC-4, the first aircraft to fly across the Atlantic Ocean, in 1919. The entire span of naval aviation history, in war and peace, is represented in the museum's remarkable collection.

I visited the museum when it was first opened in 1962. Its mission is to preserve Navy, Marine, and Coast Guard aviation history, and to exhibit for future generations some of the aircraft associated with hallowed Navy exploits. I went back again in the 1970s and was delighted to find the progress that had been made. I recently visited the museum again. It is truly a landmark achievement. It is home to the finest collection of naval aircraft from the past ninety years and, along with accompanying exhibits, stands as a monument to naval aviation heroes and pioneers.

Everything is there, from the days of the Wright brothers to the Space Age, a veritable showcase of flying nostalgia, including flight logs, vintage instruments, regulation flying apparel, and mementos from actual events and battles. There is a tribute to the recipients of the Naval Medal of Honor, and the prestigious Hall of Honor recognizes the accomplishments of nearly fifty aviation pioneers. Many scale models of aircraft, dirigibles, and spacecraft complement a dozen model aircraft carriers that represent virtually every class of carrier from the first, the USS *Langley*, to the nuclear-powered USS *Enterprise*.

On November 14, 1910, pioneer aviator Eugene Ely took off in a biplane from a specially built platform on USS *Birmingham*, a Navy cruiser. He flew to a beach two miles away. Based on this test, the Navy embarked on its commitment to aviation, and in doing so formed a new element in sea power.

In the summer of 1989 the museum was designated a "national institution," sharing that exclusive status with the U.S. Air Force Museum at Dayton, Ohio, and the

Smithsonian Air and Space Museum in Washington, D.C. These are the only three federally sanctioned air-and-space museums in America.

There is glamour everywhere in the museum, as well as history and records of deeds of valor. There is a great deal of space and the planes and exhibits are artfully displayed. Perhaps the most impressive sight in the state-of-the-art building is the seven-story glass-and-steel Greater Pensacola Blue Angel Atrium, the museum's ceremonial center, site of a dazzling aerial display featuring four A-4 Skyhawks—once flown by the Blue Angels—suspended from the ceiling in diamond formation about forty feet above the museum floor.

THE FIRST AIRCRAFT purchased by the Navy, in 1911, was called the A-1 Triad. There is a reproduction of this plane in the museum, which, although it is the only non-authentic item on display, has been meticulously reconstructed from the original plans.

Probably one of the best known aircraft in the world is the F-14 Tomcat jet fighter. The first Tomcat ever placed on public display graces the museum's entrance, while a second is displayed on the museum's flight line.

There is also on display a similar model of the torpedo bomber that former president George Bush was flying when he was shot down in the Pacific in World War II. A Stearman trainer actually flown by President Bush during WWII is on display, along with the president's log book.

Here, too, is an F6F Hellcat, the type of plane that is credited with scoring 75 percent of the total Navy and Marine air-to-air combat victories in World War II; and the F-4 Phantom II, a jet combat fighter with a top speed of 1,500 mph, which at one time or another held every operational tactical aircraft record. A full range of Navy and Marine helicopters is in the museum, including the famous minesweeper, the CH-53A Sea Stallion.

The Space Age is represented by a Skylab Command Module, in which an all-Navy crew traveled to the orbiting Skylab space station and returned to earth after twenty-eight days in space; an exact replica of the Apollo spacesuit worn by astronaut Navy Captain Eugene Cernan, the last man to set foot on the moon; a replica of the lunar rover used by the Apollo 17 crew during their mission to the moon; a Mercury space capsule

Ready to pounce with jet-fast claws, this F-14 Tomcat is on permanent display.

Treat for adults and children alike, the life-size flight deck of USS *Cabot*, a World War II aircraft carrier.

The legendary NC-4, first plane to cross the Atlantic.

Photo by Starr Smith.

similar to the one used by Navy aviator Alan Shepard, the first American in space, who also went on to walk on the moon on Apollo 12. The first man to walk on the moon was Neil Armstrong, also a Navy flier.

And in vivid contrast to the high-tech advances of the space age, there is a World War II Jeep used by the Marines in their island-hopping victories in the Pacific.

IDEALLY LOCATED ON THE legendary Pensacola Naval Air Station close to Pensacola Bay, and surrounded by thirty-seven wooded acres, the museum facility includes the South Wing, West Wing, the Blue Angel Atrium, the Museum Store, Cubi Bar Cafe, and, importantly, an IMAX® Theatre, restoration area, and outdoor aircraft exhibits. The museum grounds lend themselves well to picnics; full handicapped access to all exhibits is provided, and there is plenty of onsite parking. There is no admission charge; the museum is free to the public.

The museum was started in the early 1960s, the dream of a small group of Naval aviators who realized that much of their history was either undocumented or, worse, falling victim to the scrap heap. Beginning with a few aircraft and small exhibits housed in a temporary wooden structure, the idea grew into its present status as one of the largest aviation museums in the world. Every year since 1997, more than a million people have visited the museum. It is the most visited museum in Florida, and since 1997 has been ranked by the Florida Division of Tourism as one of the state's top ten attractions.

In 1996 the museum completed its most recent addition: a $14 million, 41,000 square foot project that added a new entrance hall and the 539-seat IMAX theater. On the Quarterdeck, as the entrance hall is known, the heroic bronzes of *The Spirit of Naval Aviation* mark five pivotal periods in the history of this unique arm of America's defense. Visitors may also see either of two films in the theater, including the museum's signature film, *The Magic of Flight*, which features an inside-the-cockpit replication of maneuvers by the Navy's world famous Blue Angels flight demonstration squadron.

The Cubi Bar Cafe offers an upscale luncheon menu and a trip through naval aviation history at a very reasonable price. Reconstructed using memorabilia from the original famous officers club at Cubi Point Naval Air Station in the Philippines, the restaurant's decor features more than a thousand squadron, ship, and unit plaques that had been presented to the club by appreciative customers during its forty years of operation. The plaques represent the work of Philippine artisans and the imagination of naval aviators, all displayed exactly as they had been when the famous club was closed in 1992.

NAVAL AVIATORS HAVE trained at the Pensacola air station for their Wings of Gold since 1914. The Blue Angels team is based in Pensacola, and former military flyers, now on the volunteer staff, conduct guided tours throughout the museum. The National Aviation Museum Foundation administers the museum and funding is provided by private and public money raised by the Foundation.

In his *Lectures on Moral Philosophy*, the English essayist Sydney Smith wrote, "To whatever height we may carry human knowledge, I hope we shall never forget those energetic and enterprising men who met the difficulty in its rudest shape." That is both the creed and the purpose of the National Museum of Naval Aviation.

For more information, contact the National Museum of Naval Aviation, 1750 Radford Blvd, Suite C, N.A.S. Pensacola, FL 32508. Phone (850) 452-3604 or (800) 327-5002. Web site www.naval-air.org.

The Alabama Shakespeare Festival
The Bard Lives On, in a Magnificent Setting

ON THAT FAIR, COLD, and memorable December day in 1985 when the Alabama Shakespeare Festival opened in Montgomery, the film and stage star Tony Randall, who was master of ceremonies, said, "It's a glorious day for the Bard. . . . I've seen all the great Shakespearean houses on earth and there is none that compares to this." And the gracious and serene Olivia de Haviland, a star in the film *Gone with the Wind*, commented, "You cannot imagine the joy and honor it is for me to be here for the dedication of this beautiful, beautiful theatre. . . . What a gift it is to Montgomery, to Alabama, to the Southeast, and to the nation."

Later the national press joined the chorus of discovery and admiration. The *Atlanta Journal-Constitution* wrote, "Truly, the Alabama Shakespeare Festival is for all seasons." *USA Today* said, "Shakespeare's a smash in Alabama." The *Boston Globe* called it "a superb theatre." The *Christian Science Monitor* complimented, "Superb productions, lavishly staged." And the good gray *New York Times* let down its hair to call the new theatre "brash and brilliant."

The Alabama Shakespeare Festival anchors the Wynton M. Blount Cultural Park, a lush and verdant oasis on the eastern edge of Montgomery. Since its opening, the Festival has staged hundreds of distinctive productions, generously laced with Shakespearean masterpieces and other plays, some with Southern backgrounds, and featuring national actors and directors of the first rank. Every year more than 200,000 people from all American states and many foreign countries, and the number is constantly

The Alabama Shakespeare Festival, Montgomery's cultural masterpiece, produces world-class plays by the Bard and other playwrights year-round.
Photo by Starr Smith.

Winton "Red" Blount with his wife, Carolyn, and *Gone with the Wind* star Olivia DeHaviland at the Festival's grand opening in 1985.

increasing, visit the great theatre described by the *Washington Post* as the "most opulent built since the end of World War II."

There is a happy, glowing, and appealing aura, a transcendental karma, in the romantic background of this theatre. It is a gift from the Montgomery business superstar and former U.S. postmaster general, Winton "Red" Blount, to his wife, Carolyn. In his dedication speech, Blount said:

> This theatre has been a work of love for Carolyn and me. I have been inspired by her interest and knowledge of Shakespeare, and this has guided me in my developing appreciation. It is a privilege for both of us to give this theatre to the people of the United States and to the generations of the future. It will stand as an enduring tribute of love to my wife, Carolyn, and it is my desire that it be known forever as the Carolyn Blount Theatre.

With the prevailing magnificence of the Carolyn Blount Theatre and the eternal love expressed so vividly by Blount for his wife, a keen observer could perhaps draw a parallel between the tall, distinguished, and polished Blount and the equally romantic and thoughtful Mogul Emperor Shah Jahan, who created India's Taj Mahal in 1648 and dedicated it to the memory of his wife, Mumtaz Mahal. The structures are obviously, for both men, tokens and monuments to love.

In his autobiographical book, *Doing It My Way*, published in 1996, Blount wrote, ". . . we were married December 22, 1981. It was a glorious day. Joy flooded into our lives, and the years since have been deliriously happy with growing love and a wonderful partnership. There has been no greater event in my life than my marriage to Carolyn. It has changed me enormously, opening a whole new world and a whole new way of life."

MONTGOMERY IS ACTUALLY the second home for the Alabama Shakespeare Festival. It was founded in Anniston, Alabama, in 1972, and produced quality plays, mostly Shakespeare's works, in a high school auditorium for six weeks in the summertime—with no air-conditioning. For a while all went well, but with a limited performance schedule, ASF was not generating enough revenue to pay the bills. Carolyn Blount, then Carolyn Varner, a former literature teacher and Shakespeare aficionado, drove often from Montgomery to Anniston to see the plays. She knew the ASF officials and eventually became a member of the board. With her guidance after their marriage, Red developed an interest in Shakespeare.

Therefore it was not surprising when ASF officials, facing bankruptcy, came to Montgomery to petition Blount for a bailout. After looking over their financial situation, he discovered that they owed three times more than the money they had requested from him. As he tells it in his book, "It was about that point that an idea popped into my head: I thought about the land behind my home, and I felt the Alabama Shakespeare Festival was too good for our state to lose. I also realized that ASF needed to be in a larger community in a modern facility where it could perform year-round and grow."

Then Blount, an astute businessman and new husband with a growing interest in the arts, particularly Shakespeare, made an offer. He tells about it in the book, saying to the visitors from Anniston, ". . . you are bankrupt and can't open your doors . . . you cannot continue to run a Shakespeare theatre with the high standards of excellence you want, in a six-week season with a total attendance of 20,000 annually . . . if ASF would move to Montgomery, Carolyn and I would build a theatre for its year-round use and would bail

Winton "Red" Blount with his wife, Carolyn.
Photo courtesy of Alabama Shakespeare Festival

ASF out of its debts." The next day the Anniston group agreed that ASF would move to Montgomery and the Blounts would build a theatre on 250 acres adjoining Wynfield, their country estate, only a few miles from downtown Montgomery. This agreement was reached in May 1982.

Always the decisive leader, Blount, with the enthusiastic support of Carolyn, went into action immediately. He commissioned his son Tom, an Atlanta architect, to draw up the plans, and envisioned a total cost of $4 or 5 million to build the theatre. It ended up costing upward of $22 million. Tom Blount's plans called for a design reminiscent of the work of the Renaissance architect Andrea Palladio, whose style had inspired Thomas Jefferson's Monticello. The renowned British landscape architect Russell Page was retained to design the surrounding grounds.

Defying superstition, the ASF opened in Montgomery on Friday the 13th with *A Midsummer Night's Dream* on the Festival Stage, while *The Glass Menagerie* opened in the Octagon.

A personal note: The announcement of ASF's move to Montgomery, and Blount's offer to build a multimillion-dollar theatre, was big news in Alabama and throughout the South. Shortly after the story broke, I wrote to Blount, who is an old friend of mine, and suggested that the theatre be named for Dr. Hudson Strode, the celebrated Shakespearean scholar and lecturer at the University of Alabama, where Red had been a student before World War II and where he was then chairman of the University's board of trustees. Blount replied immediately, pointing out that he and Strode were close friends, and praising Strode's formidable national reputation in the Shakespeare field. But he made no mention of my suggestion. In his book is this line: "I still hadn't told Carolyn that I was going to name the theatre for her. I was saving that as a surprise."

TODAY THE CAROLYN Blount Theatre stands in noble splendor on a gentle rise, facing a small lake where black swans move gracefully over placid waters. In the summertime, concerts are held around the lake, and people both young and old come year-round for strolling, hand-holding, and picnics. In the distance, situated in a complementary way, is the Montgomery Museum of Fine Arts, which was built as part of the theatre complex, and which is home of the Blount art collection.

The major complex of the Shakespeare Festival covers 97,000 square feet. There are two performing centers, or theatres, around which the Festival revolves—the Festival Stage with 750 seats, opening off the Grand Lobby, and the smaller downstairs Octagon, with a 225 seat capacity. For most of the year, both theatres feature concurrent performances. The Festival provides a more conventional theatre setting, while the informal Octagon employs a "theatre in the round" format. Perhaps the most striking single feature of the theatre is a larger-than-life statue of William Shakespeare that commands the Grand Lobby. This is a replica of the statue in New York City's Central Park, created in 1870 by John Quincy Adams Ward. The casting for the replica was done by Vanessa Hoheb, the same artist who made the casting for the recent restoration work on the Statue of Liberty.

Looking back now over the years since 1985 and the resounding success of the Alabama Shakespeare Festival, it is well to recall the prophetic words of Blount at the outset, "We are building a theatre second to none to provide the finest Shakespeare in this land and beyond." Perhaps stemming from Blount's striking and magnetic personality, his ability to recognize and act on a fortuitous opportunity, and the fabulous success of his companies in the arena of global contracting and manufacturing, the Alabama Shakespeare Festival has moved forward with purpose, focus, and, at times, daring strides. And it has not pulled away from cultivating rich new ground. Taking a cue from a line in *Twelfth Night*, its credo could well be, "Be not afraid of greatness; some are born great, some achieve greatness, and some have greatness thrust upon them."

Generally, the ASF mounts twelve to fifteen plays on the boards at both the Festival Stage and the Octagon each year. Typically, in the latter part of 2001 will be produced two Shakespeare offerings, *Julius Caesar* and *King John*, Noel Coward's *Relative Values*, Oscar Wilde's *An Ideal Husband*, *The Princess and the Black-eyed Pea*, and the world premiere of a Southern Writers' Project creation, *The Negro of Peter the Great*.

ARTISTIC DIRECTOR OF the Alabama Shakespeare Festival, and responsible for all of its productions, is Mississippi-born Kent Thompson. With credits in England, Canada, and throughout the United States, few figures can match his impressive and diversified accomplishments. Thompson has directed more than half of the entire Shakespearean canon, including *Othello, Macbeth, Antony and Cleopatra, Hamlet, The Tempest,* and *The Merchant of Venice,* and is viewed as one of the most versatile directors in the world. He has directed at the Cleveland Playhouse, North Carolina Shakespeare Festival, Boston Shakespeare Company, Studio Arena Theatre, Stage West, and is a past president of the Theatre Communications Group, the national organization for not-for-profit professional theatre. Thompson is a Phi Beta Kappa graduate of the College of William and Mary, with further training at the Juilliard School, Temple University, the University of Washington, Boston University, and the University of North Carolina School for the Arts.

Thompson points to his Southern heritage as background and early training for his eclectic and productive career. He says:

> Born and raised in the South, I know the value of a good story. All my life, people have been telling me stories, both true and false—or, should I say, some real and some invent-

Medieval Gardens is part of the growing ASF complex.

Photo by Starr Smith.

119

ed. Family holidays always began with "talk marathons," when we told the news and recited, like a ritual, favorite old family stories. My mother's family were French Huguenot–from-Virginia-to-Kentucky farmers; the desired outcome of their stories seemed to be laughter and occasionally tears. My father's family were Tennessee Scottish-Irish horse trainers and farmers. Everyone tended to talk at once at the top of her or his voice. As far as I could figure, the purpose of these stories was amazement and wonder. My grandfather told whoppers—tales of family heroics or outlandish achievement spun ever higher, in the ancient tradition of both Appalachia and medieval Europe.

Beyond that, my father told stories professionally. His were spiritual and frequent, because he was a Southern Baptist preacher. Every week he stood before thousands and undertook a remarkable feat—part worship, part exhortation, part seduction, and part inspiration. . . .

Then there was my fascination with Southern literature. My mother led me first to the great Southern storytellers, from Eudora Welty to Walker Percy, Tennessee Williams to Lillian Hellmann, Mark Twain to William Faulkner . . .

Kent Thompson is not only a brilliant theatrical director and producer, he is also a thinker, planner, visionary, and above all an innovator who makes his dreams come true. Moreover, he is a Southerner, who recognizes the wellspring of Faulkner, Williams, Welty, Capote, and Thomas Wolfe. Thus in his quest for meaningful regional plays has come the creation at ASF of the Southern Writers' Project. Here is the way Thompson tells it:

There were so many virtues to ASF—its mission to produce the works of the world's greatest playwright, a talented acting company, and a wonderfully supportive board of directors—but there was nothing in our programming to reflect the region that had created this theatre . . .

If we could create new Southern plays, I knew the audience would recognize immediately and vividly the characters, settings, and situations in these stories. I believed that our Southern stories would inform and enhance our Shakespeare stories, and vice versa. Who could not experience *King Lear* with greater depth after seeing *Cat on a Hot Tin Roof?*

We have created the Southern Writers' Project to commission new plays by and/or about Southerners. This undertaking has brought many, many wonderful stories that are now finding their ways onto stages across the country: *Lizard, Thunder Knocking on the Door, Ain't Got Long to Stay Here, Grover, The Coming of Rain*, and *The Moving of Lila Barton*. And many, many more will follow: *Fair and Tender Ladies, Lurleen, A Lesson Before Dying*.

Artistic Director Kent Thompson and the statue of the Bard in the theatre lobby.

Photo courtesy of ASF/Scarsbrook.

Certainly, with an artistic director of Thompson's precision and exactitude, the actor is the primary focus. Thompson says, "When the human story is the most important element in creating a play, it means that the actor and his or her performance are the most important parts."

Thompson's actors have the benefit of working with voice and movement coaches; full rehearsal schedules provide ample time to develop their roles. Most casting is done in New York, and ASF players are Actors Equity members. Over the years a number of top-flight players have become tremendous favorites and return season after season, to the point that they form a permanent company. These favorites include Greta Lambert, Philip Pleasants, Ray Chambers, Barry Boys, Rodney Clark, Greg Thornton, and others. For example, when Greta Lambert and Phillip Pleasants act in a play, a full house is assured. The ASF has built that sort of reputation.

STRIVING ALWAYS TO reach out to all of Alabama and the surrounding states, the ASF developed a plan several years ago to encourage weekend visitors to come to Montgomery for professional theatre. Working with the motels and hotels in the nearby area, a package deal was put together whereby playgoers could have a weekend of theatre—Friday night, Saturday matinee and night, and sometimes a matinee on Sunday. In short, a three or four play weekend that has proven quite enticing. It is not unusual to see auto license plates from many Southern states in the parking areas.

Another popular feature of the ASF extension program, and one that is dear to the hearts of Red, Carolyn, Kent Thompson, and all involved with the Festival, is the SchoolFest. This is a student-matinee program enabling school groups to enjoy performances at greatly reduced prices. The SchoolFest brings in 40,000 schoolchildren from Alabama and other states every year.

Patti Sumner, head of the Alabama Travel Council, has told me that the Alabama Shakespeare Festival is the number one cultural attraction in Alabama, and is in the top five among the most popular overall tourist attractions in the state. Mike Sherman, business writer for the *Montgomery Advertiser*, has reported that the ASF is the fifth-largest Shakespeare festival in the world, and the only year-round professional classical repertory theatre in the Southeast.

Over and above the popularity of the ASF, the Wynton M. Blount Cultural Park, from the beginning in the 1980s, has been an extraordinary serene, wooded, year-round leisure-time retreat. The mayor of Montgomery, Bobby Bright, has said, "Over time, this will be one of the most beautiful backyards in America, attracting thousands of tourists and visitors." With the Carolyn Blount Theatre as the centerpiece, standing majestically on the lake, the park covers 250 acres. The nearby Museum of Fine Arts is itself quite a tourist attraction.

In the late 1990s the Blounts decided to expand the park to 300 acres to include their home, Wynfield, and many other beguiling attractions. Plans call for sculptures, a wood and stone bridge, another lake, and an English village with a pub-restaurant. When completed in 2002, there will be a winding road that will run between the Festival and the Museum of Fine Art and through the park, skirting three lakes, crossing a wooden bridge, and connecting two Montgomery streets.

Already completed, and a major part of the park's development, is the Shakespeare Garden and Amphitheatre, hard by the Festival. It is one of seven such major gardens in America and features plants and flowers that are mentioned in Shakespeare's plays, such as roses from *Romeo and Juliet*, narcissus from *Antony and Cleopatra*, and lavender from *The Winter's Tale*. The thatched roof of the Garden pavilion, using Turkish water reeds and English combed wheat, is a striking contrast to the formal Carolyn Blount Theatre next door.

Just as the existing Festival was a $23 million dollar gift by the Blounts, the innovative addition to the Wynton M. Blount Cultural Park is being underwritten entirely by the Blount family and the Blount Foundation, which was established in 1970. At that time Red Blount said, "One of the great strengths of the American people has been their resolve to support organizations and activities designed to serve the general welfare. The Blount Foundation was created to serve as a voice to address the need to provide financial assistance to activities and programs concerned with the general welfare of our country and its citizens." President of the Foundation is Blount's longtime right-hand man, confidante, and former top executive with the Blount companies, Joe McInnes, who is a native of nearby Wetumpka and a graduate of the University of Alabama. The astute and personable McInnes points out that the Foundation supports health, education, civic affairs, and cultural activities.

RED BLOUNT, before the 1999 sale of Blount International, his global New York Stock Exchange company, and his subsequent transition to full-time development of the Cultural Park, was one of America's premier businessmen, as well as serving as President Richard Nixon's postmaster general and heading the United States Chamber of Commerce. Among other major projects, his companies built the Titan missile launch pads at Cape Canaveral, the New Orleans Superdome, and a $2 billion dollar university in Saudi Arabia. Yet he is tremendously proud of the fact that he was born and reared in the unlikely setting of Union Springs, Alabama.

Moreover, his passion for culture and the arts, and his dedication toward making art treasures available to all the people, can be summed up in his own words: "If history is to be the judge of our achievement as a nation, what will it say about those who would determine that art was merely an indulgence of the wealthy; that the whole people did not need it, and ought to be denied it by reason of their means? . . . I was raised to believe—and, in my final years, continue to embrace the proposition—that a nation advances and grows strong by allocating its opportunities not to *some* of its people, but to *all* of them . . .

Nothing could be more wonderful for Carolyn and me than to see people responding to what we've done here. I tell my friends around the country: don't wait until you're dying to give something. Give it now so you can be part of it."

Allen Tate, the American poet and critic, has some defining and convincing words on the subject of culture. He said, "Culture is the study of perfection and the constant effort to achieve it." Red Blount is now approaching his eightieth year. And in many years of seeking, embracing, encouraging, and promoting art and culture for the people of Alabama and the South, certainly he has not achieved perfection. But he has indubitably sown the seeds and pointed the way. He is widely respected and honored throughout the South, and deeply revered in his hometown of Montgomery. In 1999, *Montgomery Living* magazine called Blount "Montgomery's Man of the Century." Rod Frazer, past chairman of the Montgomery Chamber of Commerce, has said, "I regard Red Blount as Montgomery's foremost citizen of the twentieth century in business and culture."

Perhaps Shakespeare spoke for Winton Blount in a line from the play *Coriolanus*: "I have lived to see inherited my very wishes and the buildings of my fancy."

And in the Spring of 2001, the *Montgomery Advertiser* published an unprecedented fourteen-page tribute to Blount, featuring a full-page cover picture. It was the first time in the 172-year history of the Pulitzer Prize–winning newspaper that an individual had been honored in such fashion. The story traced Blount's life from his days in Union Springs through his tremendous success as an international businessman, president's cabinet member, and University of Alabama trustee. But by far the main thrust of this remarkable tribute centered on his contribution to culture and the arts, and the Alabama Shakespeare Festival and its impact in the South. In an editorial in the special Blount section, the *Advertiser* stated: "His most visible contribution is the Alabama Shakespeare Festival, a theatre facility widely recognized as one of the finest in the world. It is a gem of the highest quality . . . its value as an entertainment and educational facility is beyond calculation."

For more information, contact the Alabama Shakespeare Festival, One Festival Drive, Montgomery, AL 36117. Phone (334) 271-5353 or (334) 841-4ASF. Web site www.asf.net/asf.html.

Breakfast at Brennan's

Owen Brennan's Famous Restaurant on Royal Street

THE FIRST TIME I was introduced to that singular New Orleans tradition and phenomenon known as Breakfast at Brennan's was on a New Year's Day in the early 1960s. I remember it well for several reasons, one of which was I had brought my daughter, Sandra Starr, then 16 or 17, on her first trip to New Orleans as a grownup. Another reason for the trip was that Alabama was playing Arkansas in the Sugar Bowl at the old Tulane Stadium. We all had a grand time. Alabama won the game; I think the score was 10-3.

But there is only one Breakfast at Brennan's, and the memory of it is as fresh as Brennan's newly baked French bread, and as crisp as that New Year's Day there on Royal Street.

Perhaps only in glorious New Orleans is there a restaurant that is one of the world's top culinary establishments, and at the same time one of the world's most famous—because quality and fame do not always go hand in hand when it comes to restaurants, but the two come together magnificently at Brennan's. The restaurant was founded by the late Owen Edward Brennan, Sr., and is today operated by his sons, Owen Jr. (or "Pip"), Jimmy, and Ted. (Brennan's Restaurant on Royal Street is not connected in any way with another branch of the fabled Brennan family, described in another chapter of this book, who operate Commander's Palace and several other New Orleans restaurants.)

Sons gather around father's portrait—(left to right) Owen Jr. ("Pip"), Ted, and Jimmy now own Brennan's. By tradition, at least one of them is always on the premises at the restaurant.

OLD-TIMERS WILL TELL YOU that never in the storied history of New Orleans has there been a more charismatic, colorful, and accomplished man than Owen Edward Brennan, Sr., who died in 1955. Some say he was the prime mover in the tremendous surge in tourism in New Orleans after World War II, largely because of his friendship with leading media figures and Hollywood stars. Others tell you that the affable and popular

126

Irishman was the city's foremost promoter of French-Creole cuisine. All agree that he was responsible for the best known and most exciting three words in New Orleans restaurant lexicon—Breakfast at Brennan's.

The senior Mr. Brennan began his hospitality career as the owner of the famed Old Absinthe House on Bourbon Street, built in 1798, and once known as the secret hangout of the pirate Jean Lafitte. In Owen Brennan's first attention-getting project, he posed lifelike mannequins of President Andrew Jackson and the notorious Lafitte in what he called the "Secret Room"—the very room in which they supposedly made a pact for the city's defense against the British at the Battle of New Orleans during the War of 1812.

The great jazz pianist Fats Pichon added to the allure and charm of Old Absinthe House.

In due course, both residents and visiting celebrities made the bar at that restaurant their favorite rendezvous: Walt Disney, actresses Vivien Leigh and Barbara Stanwyck, actors John Wayne, Gary Cooper, Robert Mitchum, and Robert Taylor, playwright Tennessee Williams, writers Walter Winchell, Earl Wilson, Hedda Hopper, Robert Ruark, Lucius Beebe, and the columnists of the local *Times-Picayune* and *New Orleans Item*. Articles about the dynamic and bright senior Mr. Brennan appeared in *Newsweek*, *Life*, *Holiday*, *Gourmet*, and other national magazines.

Meantime he had moved across Bourbon Street and in 1946 opened his first restaurant named after himself, Owen Brennan's Vieux Carre. It became an instant success and competed with New Orleans's oldest and best restaurants in French and Creole cuisine.

The senior Mr. Brennan had no training in the restaurant business, but his vivid imagination, creative ability, constant hard work, and instincts to hire the right professional help, paved the way to success.

About this time the best-selling novel *Dinner at Antoine's* by Frances Parkinson Keyes came out. Always on the alert for new and catchy public relations and marketing concepts, the Keyes novel sparked the idea for the phrase "Breakfast at Brennan's," which rapidly became a popular tradition at Vieux Carre.

The year 1955 turned out to be fateful for the senior Mr. Brennan. Due to leasing disagreements on Bourbon Street, he decided to move his restaurant to another location, still in the French Quarter, at 417 Royal Street. He set to renovating and redecorating the historic old building, which was constructed in 1795 as a lavish mansion.

Official opening of the restaurant was scheduled for the spring of 1956. Before that joyful occasion could take place, the senior Mr. Brennan died of a heart attack in November 1955. He was forty-five years old. His wife, Maude, the three sons, Pip, Jimmy, and Ted, and other members of the extended Brennan family opened the new restaurant and operated it together until the sons assumed sole ownership in 1974. They then established a tradition that there is at least one Brennan on the premises at all times, day or night. So whenever you go to Brennan's, Pip, Jimmy, or Ted will always be on hand.

The advancement of the New Orleans tourist community was high on Owen Brennan, Sr.'s list of priorities. He was labeled a "one-man chamber of commerce" and his highest interest was promoting tourism. Appointed by Mayor Chep Morrison, Brennan was the founding chairman of the first New Orleans Tourism Commission and was a driving force in the city Chamber of Commerce. As a major promoter of the New Orleans tourism industry, Brennan once arranged a special Mardi Gras ball for visitors in town during the Carnival season.

With the possible exception of New York mayors Jimmy Walker and Fiorello LaGuardia, no man in America has done more to make his city attractive and enticing to visitors than Owen Brennan did for New Orleans. Furthermore, Walker and LaGuardia

Front entrance of Brennan's, the most famous restaurant in the South and a symbol of New Orleans itself.
Photo by Starr Smith.

were powerful officeholders with vast resources. Brennan was not an elected official, but he did have a passionate love for his town, and the vision and imagination to see its tourism possibilities. Perhaps most important, many of his friends were highly placed in the media; they publicized New Orleans—and Brennan's restaurant—with boundless enthusiasm.

With the vivacious and high-spirited Jill Jackson, a well-known radio personality, Brennan produced and cohosted a late Friday night interview program broadcast on WWL, a 50,000 watt clear-channel radio station. The broadcast, which featured visiting celebrities, originated from Brennan's restaurant and was heard all over the South. The guests, needing little prompting, extolled the pleasures and attractions of New Orleans.

When Owen Brennan died, both New Orleans newspapers, the *Times-Picayune* and *Item*, ran banner headlines, and *Time* magazine noted his death in its "Milestones" column. The *Times-Picayune* obituary read, "There was something wonderfully winning about this man . . . and the happy-hearted way in which he built his restaurant into a famous institution, competing with the city's oldest and best French and Creole cuisine . . . New Orleans tourist business was part of Brennan's trade. But it was more than that with him— it was his great enthusiasm. His interest in making this the greatest resort center of the South extended far beyond the walls of Brennan's Restaurant."

THE RESTAURANT TODAY occupies three floors in the old mansion, with twelve handsomely decorated dining rooms, a bar, and an outside courtyard. It is open for breakfast, brunch, lunch, and dinner seven days a week from 8 A.M. to 10 P.M., closed only on Christmas Eve night and Christmas Day. It has been called one of the ten best American restaurants by former Parisian Art Buchwald, and named Louisiana's No. 1 restaurant by *Louisiana Life* magazine. The wine cellar is perhaps the best in the South from Houston to Tampa.

Since my first visit to Brennan's, I've gone back many times, and it is still thrilling to turn in off Royal Street and walk down the long entranceway, past the bar, and onto the patio.

Brennan's serves more than a thousand people every day. The longtime and renowned chef is Mike Roussel, who recommends that guests coming for Breakfast at

Owen Brennan, founder of Brennan's Restaurant and a pioneer in the promotion of tourism in New Orleans.

Photo courtesy of Brennan's Restaurant.

Brennan's should allow themselves plenty of time, since the great culinary occasion can take two or three hours.

A typical Brennan's Breakfast starts with an eye-opener—Brandy Milk Punch or Creole Bloody Mary. Then, as Mike planned it for me recently, we moved along to Southern Baked Apple with Double Cream; a Brennan original—Eggs Hussarde, poached eggs atop Holland rusks, Canadian bacon, and Marchand de Vin sauce, topped with Hollandaise sauce, and, of course, served with Brennan's Hot French Bread. The dessert was the acclaimed Brennan's Bananas Foster, bananas sautéed in butter, brown sugar, cinnamon, and banana liqueur, then flamed in rum, and served over vanilla ice cream. It's traditional to have wine with Breakfast at Brennan's, and Mike came forward with a crisp Pouilly Fuisse. As a favor to me, Mike started with another Brennan trademark—spicy thick turtle soup, and, being a Southern boy, I asked for a side order of grits. At the end, there was that addictive New Orleans coffee.

Few restaurants in the world have captured international attention and held it with dedication, permanence, and élan quite as well as Brennan's on Royal Street has done for more than fifty years. Just as Owen Sr. had a gilt-edged relationship with the media giants of his day—Walter Winchell, Lucius Beebe, Robert Ruark, Hedda Hopper and others—the sons know a thing or two about public relations. Betty Guillaud, the celebrated columnist of the *Times-Picayune* and one of the most widely read and quoted local writers in America, gives the Brennan boys high marks for so brilliantly carrying on their father's storied tradition. But, of course, the essential element is a product of the first rank—the restaurant itself. Here are a few random newspaper and magazine quotes. *Southern Living* wrote:

> Dinner by candlelight at a white-tablecloth restaurant is often the choice for a special occasion. But in New Orleans, who needs to wait for sunset? "Breakfast at Brennan's" has been a be-all, end-all, budget-busting celebration for decades.

Life put it briefly, "First-timers to New Orleans absolutely should sample Bananas Foster at Brennan's." *Bon Appetit* elevated the restaurant to institutional status, as viewed by writer Tom Fitzmorris: "Breakfast at Brennan's is a unique culinary landmark. There could hardly be a more pleasant place to start the day."

Focus, the New Orleans city business publication, wrote:

> For a half century, the sunset-colored walls of Brennan's Restaurant have drawn locals and tourists, the rich and the not-so-rich, into a small world of elegance in the French Quarter . . . Brennan's seemed charmed from the beginning. Since its founding, the restaurant has been "where one goes" when in New Orleans.

Brennan's is expensive. But the *New Orleans Times-Picayune* "Lagniappe" column put it this way: "Brennan's is no place for the budget-conscious . . . But those dollars go to buy some of the finest prime beef and fresh seafood available, and help stock a huge wine cellar second to none in New Orleans." Associated Press writer Mary MacVean quotes Ted Brennan: "Out-of-town visitors come to Brennan's all the time. But New Orleans people come on weekends. It would be hard to go to work after a three-hour breakfast with eye-openers and wine."

John Mariani, the restaurant columnist for *Esquire* magazine, likes Brennan's, and it came through in this story:

> Combine New Orleans's legendary hospitality with an infectious Irish spirit and you have Brennan's. With its spectacular wine list, its lush courtyard, and its fine traditional Creole and French cuisine, Brennan's is one of the most impressive and elegant restaurants in the French Quarter and the food has never been better.

And in a glowing review, Donna Lou Morgan, the food editor of the *Tampa Tribune*, wrote: "The 'Grand Creole Breakfast' was invented at Brennan's Restaurant in the French Quarter in New Orleans about fifty years ago. That meal has made the restaurant famous. With good cause."

IN HONOR OF THEIR FATHER on the fiftieth anniversary of the restaurant, the Brennan sons—Owen Jr. (Pip), Jimmy, and Ted—published an elegant and well-turned-out book, *Breakfast at Brennan's and Dinner, Too.* On that occasion, Eleanor Ostman of the *St. Paul Pioneer Press* stated: "If there is anything lacking in the book, otherwise as comely as a Mardi Gras queen, it is that the reader is left longing for more."

Brennan's in New Orleans is a unique Southern treasure. No visitor—or anyone else—in the Crescent City should miss it, for breakfast or any other occasion. It will leave you longing for more.

For more information, contact Brennan's Restaurant, 417 Royal St., New Orleans, LA 70130-2191. Phone (504) 525-9711, fax (504) 525-2302. Web site www.brennansrestaurant.com

Callaway Gardens
One Family's Gift of Beauty and Nature

JUST OUTSIDE THE Virginia Hand Callaway Discovery Center is a wrought-iron sign that states simply:

> Take nothing from the Gardens
> except Nourishment for the Soul,
> Consolation for the Heart, and
> Inspiration for the Mind.

This is the credo and guiding light of one of the most beautiful and incomparable scenes on this earth—Callaway Gardens.

While this unique resort has a fine hotel, guest cottages, superb food, golf, tennis, more than a dozen lakes, a manmade beach, walking paths, a circus, bicycle trails, butterflies, swimming pools, flowers in brilliant profusion, towering stands of oak and pine trees, a horse race, a world-class *Christmas Festival in Lights*, and all the other graceful amenities of the good vacation life—Callaway Gardens has something more. Perhaps it is an aura, maybe a state of mind. But all the things found in such rich abundance at Callaway Gardens add up to a resort of the first rank and rare distinction, that draws more than one million visitors a year to this oasis in the rolling hills of west central Georgia.

Callaway Gardens, seventy miles southwest of Atlanta, is a magical setting for all people in all seasons. In springtime, the Gardens become a glorious blanket of flowers and

Best-selling author Dick Francis at a signing event for his book *Wild Horses* at Callaway Gardens.

Photo by Starr Smith.

greenery, highlighted by Spring Celebration Weekends, an annual Plant Fair, and Celebrate the Arts Weekend. In the summertime, the Flying High Circus of Florida State University performs every day, followed by the Labor Day weekend, with more high-flying fun at the Sky High Hot Air Balloon Festival.

In autumn, the Buick Challenge PGA golf tournament is played on Callaway's Mountain View course, and the world famous Steeplechase is held in November. Because of its mild climate, Callaway welcomes many visitors for winter vacations. Christmas brings America's brightest outdoor illuminated show, with more than three million glittering Yuletide lights spaced along a winding eight-mile trail through the Gardens. It is the celebrated Callaway Gardens Christmas gift to the Southland, *Fantasy in Lights*.

Easter time is also special at the Gardens, and year-round there is the fascination of the Sibley Horticultural Center, the Day Butterfly Center, and, now, the Virginia Hand Callaway Discovery Center.

136

DREAMS DO NOT always come true in this world. Callaway Gardens is a dream that did. It has reached the full scope of its founder's thoughts, plans, and vision. Who among us could have imagined that, in less than fifty years, a holiday haven of such exquisite beauty and vibrant excitement could emerge from Georgia cotton fields and rambling woodlands.

International Steeplechase is held every November.
Photo by Starr Smith.

"Every child ought to see something beautiful before he's six years old—something he would remember the rest of his life. All I've done is to fix it so that anybody who came to the Gardens would see something beautiful wherever he might look." These are the words of Cason Callaway, an industrialist from nearby La Grange, who with his wife, Virginia Hand Callaway, took vacations at Blue Springs, Georgia, near Pine Mountain.

Bo Callaway, the Gardens' hands-on chairman, seen here visiting a recent expansion project.

The time was the 1930s, the years of the Great Depression, when there was little beauty in America, except the natural kind found in their part of the South.

Cason Callaway's father was the founder of the Callaway Textile Mills, but in Cason's heart of hearts he was a man of the soil, a farmer. Thus it was in those somber Depression days that the Callaways began to revitalize the area, to project their vision and move forward with their dream to, in their words, "restore and preserve the natural surroundings near Pine Mountain, to protect native species of plant and animal life there, and provide the general public with a beautiful garden setting for education, inspiration, and recreation."

The Callaways worked for many years to carry out this dictum and create their dream place. They gave new life to worn-out cotton fields, dammed streams to make lakes and control erosion, and collected and planted native and exotic flowers, trees, and shrubs.

In 1951 the Callaways deeded the property to the Ida Cason Callaway Foundation, named for Mr. Callaway's mother. In 1952 the state of Georgia chartered the Gardens as an "educational, horticultural, and charitable institution." Later in 1952, Callaway Gardens opened its gates to the public. The people liked it—more than fifty thousand came that first year.

Since those early days, thirty million people have visited the Gardens, which are operated, as their literature states, ". . . for the benefit of mankind . . . to combine a man-made landscape within a natural setting where all may find beauty, relaxation, inspiration, and a better understanding of the living world." Truly, the original goal that the Callaways set for themselves and their remarkable endeavor has been achieved.

CALLAWAY GARDENS is a multipurpose internationally famous resort, wildlife preserve, flowering woodland, and animal sanctuary. It spreads over more than fourteen thousand acres of Georgia countryside. It has so many enticing features that it is difficult to pinpoint them all, but two stand out as major attractions for everyone, and especially for families: the John A. Sibley Horticultural Center and the Cecil B. Day Butterfly Center.

The Butterfly Center is the home of more than a thousand butterflies. It is a 7,000-foot habitat filled with fifty species of tropical butterflies. The environment is created especially for their benefit. The center is the largest free-flight, glass-enclosed conservatory in North America. Butterflies are everywhere, in all of their magnificent and dazzling colors—take pictures of them if you are quick enough. Every element of the octagonal building encourages the butterflies, tropical plants, and guests to interact with the natural surroundings. Visitor paths bordered by foliage lead to several levels.

Outside, crowning the roof of Day Center, and indeed its focal point, is the Hand Cupola, brought from the childhood home of Virginia Hand Callaway at Pelham, Georgia, in the 1970s. The center is named for Cecil B. Day, founder of the Days Inn hotel/motel chain. In taking a leadership role in establishing the center, his widow, Mrs. Deen Day Smith of Atlanta, said, "I've always loved butterflies. The conservation of these

Ida Cason Callaway Memorial Chapel—A serene sanctuary in the heart of the Gardens. The chapel was named for the founder's mother.

beautiful creatures is important because they are rapidly disappearing from our natural surroundings."

The Sibley Horticultural Center has been called the most advanced green-house/garden complex in the world. It was named for John A. Sibley, a Georgia banker, lawyer, civic leader, and flower lover, who was a friend of the Callaway family.

Inside and outside, the Center covers five acres. It is a most unusual "greenhouse," featuring lush green lawns, exotic and native plants, seasonal flower beds, and a two-story waterfall. The Center's design is unique, and, it seemed to me, the perfect building for its purpose—modern, spacious, casual, and visitor-friendly. It lends itself to floral displays in both an indoor and outdoor setting; everything flows into an integrated pattern that is both convenient and pleasing to the eye. There are eighteen major floral displays every year.

Never far removed from his love of nature and the soil, Cason Callaway, before his death in 1961, established a modern 7.5 acre garden. It is called Mr. Cason's Vegetable Garden and it now produces more than four hundred varieties of vegetables, fruits, and herbs. It is the setting for *The Victory Garden*, a popular TV series.

Incidentally, more than seven hundred varieties of azaleas are grown in the Gardens, including the plum-leaf azalea, which was found by the Callaways growing wild in the vicinity of Pine Mountain. It now flourishes in many parts of the United States and abroad.

Perhaps the most memorable attraction at Callaway Gardens is the Ida Cason Callaway Memorial Chapel, named for the founder's mother. The lovely little sanctuary sits serenely on a wooded lake in the heart of the Gardens. It is a place for quiet meditation and worship, and organ concerts are held there.

AS CALLAWAY GARDENS nears the end of its fifth decade of glorious service, it is a world-class resort, home of 230 types of birds, 1,000 butterflies, 50 species of other wildlife, 700 different kinds of azaleas, 400 varieties of vegetables, fruits, and herbs, a vegetable garden featured on national television, and miles of natural woodland.

Surely no place is more serene and peaceful, yet activity is everywhere. There are no loud noises or untoward incidents. People come to relax, have a good time, and leave their troubles at home.

This just may be the very best place in the whole world for family vacations. A family can spread out. There is plenty of space—games, the beach, swimming pools, the circus, tennis, golf, the bicycle trail . . . the list goes on.

There are sixty-three holes of golf at Callaway, ten lighted tennis courts, two racquetball courts, skeet and trap shooting, fishing in the lakes, a fly-fishing program, and a fitness center. The Discovery Bicycle Trail, a ten-mile wooded trail, weaves through the Gardens. The golf courses include the championship Mountain View, where the Buick Challenge is played in late September, and the Sky View, Garden View, and Lake View

Large inland manmade beach, surrounded by wooded picnic grounds.

courses—a wide range of choices from moderate to difficult. Nearby is the world's largest inland manmade beach on 65-acre Robin Lake.

The Callaway Brothers Azalea Bowl has become a major attraction for flower lovers. Encompassing forty acres, the Bowl is the largest azalea garden in the world and includes a reflecting pond, gazebo, winding paths, and a babbling brook.

A welcome addition to the Gardens is the spectacular Virginia Hand Callaway Discovery Center. It was named for the cofounder of the Gardens, who was also the mother of Howard "Bo" Callaway, a former Georgia congressman and secretary of the Army, who is now chairman of Callaway Gardens.

For many years, sometimes working behind the scenes, Bo, a man of enormous talent, energy, vision, and drive, has quietly prepared Callaway Gardens for entry, as a major attraction, into the twenty-first century. He has been the keeper of his father Cason's unique dream, a garden "prettier than any since Eden." Millard Grimes, the famed Georgia editor, has written, "Under Bo's leadership Callaway Gardens has become

142

Georgia's most famous resort." According to Grimes, Bo has been successful in getting across the philosophy ". . . that Callaway Gardens is not a resort adjacent to some gardens. It *is* the Gardens, with resort facilities available."

These days, the day-by-day operation of Callaway Gardens is in the hands of Howard "Bo" Callaway, Jr., a Duke and Harvard business school graduate, who is president and CEO. But Bo Sr. is not exactly resting on his laurels as one of the South's foremost tourism and travel innovators—he lives in Pine Mountain and keeps a sharp eye on the Gardens. Now in his early seventies, he travels extensively with his wife, Beth, and spends time sailing his boat off the British Virgin Islands in the Caribbean.

The 35,000 square foot Discovery Center is nestled in the woods along the edge of Mountain Creek Lake and serves as the focal point for guests. Here an orientation theater, activities videos, interactive kiosks, and staff members provide information about the Garden's history and the wonders of the surrounding area. The Center is the scene of daily birds-of-prey shows and an auditorium for lectures, entertainment, and nature films. An exhibition hall features a variety of shows at various times during the year, and the Discovery shop is filled with many nature-related items. The Mountain Creek Cafe offers both a stunning view and excellent food.

Dining, in all of its inviting forms, is a sheer joy for the whole family at Callaway. The Plantation Room is one of the most popular restaurants at the resort. The whole experience of the Friday night seafood buffet and the Sunday brunch are so pleasant that guests remember them for a long time.

I had a cool and lovely lunch on the porch of the Gardens Restaurant, overlooking a lake and a golf course; I also had an Italian dinner at the Veranda, a casual lunch at the Flower Mill, breakfast at the Country Kitchen, and drinks and snacks at the Vineyard Green. On my last night at Callaway, I dined with a friend in the fabled Georgia Room, just off the lobby in the Inn. Not a large room, it has places for only sixty people. The tables are for four and are well spaced. I rank the Georgia Room right along with the great restaurants of Atlanta—it's that good. On the menu that night was a tempting selection of new Southern cuisine, delectable and adventurous. The wine list in the Georgia Room is extensive and offers wines in several price ranges.

Lodging at Callaway, like all features of the resort, is upscale, guest-friendly, and not excessively priced. The Inn, Callaway's centerpiece, has 349 rooms. The Callaway

Country Cottages have 155 two and three bedroom units, and the Mountain Creek Villas have 50 two, three, and four bedroom suites.

I SUPPOSE THAT THE wind blowing gently through the tall pines sets the tone at Callaway Gardens. The air seems different—pure, almost perfumelike, a balm to the senses. I have never encountered better treatment from service and staff people. They know their jobs and go out of their way to provide superior service.

Truly, the purpose of Mr. and Mrs. Callaway has been reached, as they originally said, "Callaway Gardens . . . seeks to combine manmade landscape within a natural setting, where all may find beauty, relaxation, inspiration, and a better understanding of the living world."

For more information, contact Callaway Gardens, P.O. Box 2000, Pine Mountain, GA 31822-2000, or phone 1-800-225-5292 (1-800-CALLAWAY). Web site www.callawaygardens.com.

The Brennans of New Orleans
A Personal Glimpse at America's First Family of Fine Dining

Perhaps the New Orleans super-chef Emeril Lagasse described it best when he said with admiration, a bit of reverence, and unbounded gusto, "What a family!" Lagasse, a television culinary star and famed restaurateur, was speaking of his friends and compatriots on the fabled Crescent City restaurant scene—the renowned Brennan family. From their capstone restaurant—the world-famous Commander's Palace in the landmark Garden District of New Orleans—the Brennans have emerged as America's First Family of Food. And media acclaim, food experts, and word of mouth have made Commander's Palace "the best restaurant in New Orleans . . . in America . . . in the world."

Emeril Lagasse began his culinary ascendancy as executive chef at Commander's Palace, eventually moving on to Emeril's, his own honored Creole cuisine cafe in New Orleans, and to television stardom. In speaking of the Brennans, therefore, he spoke from firsthand knowledge and pleasurable experience. And indeed, by any measuring rod, the Brennans are quite a family—in the food culture, in success in the business community, and in respect, admiration, and veneration by their peers throughout America. John Mariani, food critic for *Esquire* magazine, said, "The Brennans are like no other restaurant family."

From her vantage point at the fabulous Commander's Palace, Ella Brennan, the family matriarch, keeps a sharp and knowing eye on the ever-changing tides of the New Orleans restaurant world.

Several years ago a friend of mine, going to New Orleans for a weekend, asked for dining recommendations. "It's easy," I told him. "Just go to the Brennan places for the whole weekend—the Palace Cafe on Canal Street for Friday night dinner, BACCO for Saturday lunch, Mr. B's on Royal for Saturday night, and for a great finale, the Sunday Jazz Brunch at Commander's Palace." Now, thanks to a fast-burning second generation of Brennans, a New Orleans visitor can dine, and dine exceedingly well, at eight Brennan restaurants throughout the city.

THE BRENNANS IN NEW ORLEANS are a lot like British royalty, and in the restaurant community they are viewed as royalty. The family has now moved into a mature and enterprising second generation, and the heirs and heirs-apparent seem to be all over the place—attractive, university-educated, friendly, venturesome, ambitious, eager, and at times audacious. Moreover, they are well trained in the restaurant business, having come up through the ranks, paying their dues, and all imbued with a strong sense of family loyalty and values. This younger generation is about evenly split between men and women, and they all understand, and seek to enhance, the luster of the Brennan name.

From her strategic vantage point at Commander's Palace, which is the mother-church of the Brennan domain, Ella Brennan, the family matriarch, who has been called the queen of the Big Easy restaurants, keeps a sharp and knowing eye on the ever-changing tides of her restaurant world. Growing up in a working-class, Depression-era family— Ella was one of six children, three boys and three girls—she learned the food and hospitality business from her brother, the legendary Owen Brennan, who founded Brennan's

146

Restaurant on Royal Street (featured elsewhere in this book), and who is generally credited with putting New Orleans on world tourism maps after World War II.

Owen Brennan is now deceased. His sons run Brennan's on Royal Street, the home of the internationally famous "Breakfast at Brennan's," which Owen also created. The two branches of the Brennan family now have no business connection at all. Ella's other brothers, John (deceased) and Dick, and two sisters, Adelaide (deceased) and Dottie, and Ella herself, founded this Brennan group.

Taken from the Brennan family tree, here is the second-generation roll call—Ella Brennan, mother of Alex Brennan-Martin and Ti Martin; John Brennan, father of Ralph, Lally, and Cindy Brennan Davis; Dick Brennan, father of Dickie and of Lauren Brennan Brower; Dottie Brennan, mother of Brad, and of two other children not connected with the business. (Adelaide Brennan had no children.)

Not only is Commander's Palace one of the world's truly great restaurants, it is also ideally suited as the Brennan family's fountainhead. In a serene setting amid the stately Greek Revival mansions in the Garden District, where Mark Twain was once entertained and where Jefferson Davis spent his last days, the majestic old restaurant has an illustrious history. In 1880, Emile Commander established the only restaurant in the District. It was patronized by his distinguished neighbors, and consequently he called it Commander's Palace. By the beginning of the twentieth century the restaurant was attracting gourmets from all over the world, just as it does today.

After the split with Owen Brennan's family, Ella, Dottie, Dick, and John Brennan took over Commander's Palace in 1974. They immediately began a total renovation of the old landmark, giving a lot of attention to the kitchen, which is today the heart and focus of the restaurant. Both Creole and American heritages were closely observed in creating the distinctive Commander's Place cuisine, with seafood, meats, and—always—fresh vegetables. Dick Brennan, a Tulane graduate, conceived the celebrated Sunday Jazz Brunch, with Mardi Gras–like colored balloons, and muted jazz performed by the city's finest musicians. Flowers, conviviality, and splendid food combined to make the Commander's Palace atmosphere, ". . . like a well-run party given by old friends."

Commander's Palace has been named several times in various publications as the best restaurant in the world. It is always ranked in the top five or ten on all significant lists. And it is consistently listed with Le Cirque in New York City, Gaddi's in the Peninsula

Hotel in Hong Kong, and the vaunted showplaces of Paris and Brussels, as one of the world's premier restaurants.

FOR SEVERAL YEARS NOW, the Brennan second generation has been on the march—bright ideas, bold concepts, and new restaurants. Jim Funk, executive vice president of the Louisiana Restaurant Association, observed, "New Orleans is one of the last bastions of independent restaurants, and people like the Brennans are helping to continue that. . . . The family has organized itself to give each one a chance to use the entrepreneurial spirit that runs so strongly in the Brennan family."

Mr. B's Bistro is a perfect example. It was opened by the Brennans in 1979 as a second-generation enterprise, with Ralph and Cindy Brennan heading the team. Tom Fitzmorris, the astute New Orleans restaurant historian, has written, "It was obvious . . . that this was the place where the every-twenty-years reinvention of the New Orleans restaurant scene would take place. Warren LeRuth had done it in the 1960s, the Brennans in the 1940s, Count Arnaud in the 1920s, Jean Galatoire in the first decade of the century, Madame Begue in the 1890s, and Antoine Alciatore [Antoine's] in the 1860s. Now it was the Brennan turn again."

Fitzmorris continued, "Ella said that the standards of the food and service would be what they'd always been in Brennan restaurants, but that the whole experience would be completely informal . . . None of the trappings of the typical gourmet restaurant were there . . . As good an idea as that sounds now, it as utterly revolutionary then. When you went out to dine well, you'd expect to get—or put up with—a certain amount of ceremony. The Brennans correctly noted that this scared a large number of people away from fine dining, so they dispensed with it and just went with casual and friendly . . . When Mr. B's opened, it was the talk of the town . . . And when the flood of new restaurants came in the early 1980s, almost all of them imitated Mr. B's in one way or another . . . The restaurant that really set the standard and inspired dozens of other places like it was Mr. B's Bistro."

Mr. B's captured national attention, too; it was even featured in a Dick Tracy cartoon. And Gregory Roberts, writing in the "Lagniappe" newspaper column, stated, "The 'B' in Mr. B's Bistro stands, of course, for Brennans, the family name of the city's most

Commander's Palace in the Garden District is the "mother church" of the Ella Brennan restaurant group in New Orleans.

prominent restaurateurs . . . It's a big and bustling place, a festive setting where locals celebrate anniversaries and graduations, yet tourists feel comfortable breezing in . . ." The restaurant is at the corner of Royal and Iberville in the heart of the French Quarter, across the street from the famed Hotel Monteleone.

New Orleans purists are happy to know that Mr. B's now occupies the corner where Solari's Market once stood. For more than a hundred years, people from all over New Orleans, and out-of-town guests, came to visit Solari's, which specialized in merchandise not found elsewhere—out-of-season fruits and vegetables, rare wines and liquors, and exquisite candy and imported cookies. Solari's closed for the last time in 1965, and fourteen years later Mr. B's Bistro came to the renowned corner.

Dick Brennan, Dickie's father, Ella's brother, and one of the founders of the Brennan family restaurants.

Photo courtesy Starr Smith

IT'S HARD TO IMAGINE a better location for an upscale New Orleans restaurant than the old Werlein Music Building at 605 Canal Street, just off Royal and on the edge of the French Quarter. It was here that Dickie Brennan founded the Palace Cafe.

After the usual Brennan apprenticeship, some experience at Commander's Palace under chef Paul Prudhomme, college at LSU and Loyola, a semester in Rome, a stint at Delmonico's in Mexico City, and work with master chef Larry Forgione at An American Place in New York, Dickie traveled to the fountainhead of the culinary world—France. He studied the French language at the Institute de Francais, then headed for Paris. There he had the good fortune to cook in some of the world's greatest restaurants, including Tour d'Argent and Taillevent.

In 1985 Dickie returned to the United States and to Houston, Texas, to manage the Brennan's restaurant there. Four years later he returned to New Orleans and set about converting the historic turn-of-the-century Werlein store into a grand cafe, comparable to the ones he had known in Paris. In March 1991 the Palace Cafe opened with Dickie as managing partner for the Brennan family. At first he functioned, along with his management duties, as executive chef, seeking to capture the true flavor of New Orleans with classic and contemporary Creole-Cajun cuisine. Although the Brennans have turned out some of the world's most celebrated chefs—Emeril Lagasse, Paul Prudhomme, Gerhard Brill, and the present Commander's Palace master, Jamie Shannon—Dickie is the only Brennan with the rank of executive chef.

The entry of Palace Cafe into the New Orleans and American restaurant orbit was noted with dazzling reviews and widespread national tribute. *Esquire* magazine and *USA*

Today came forward with Best New Restaurant awards for 1991. Throughout the decade of its existence, Palace Cafe has continued to gain honors year after year, including the *Great Chefs* TV series; the New Orleans Restaurant of the Year award; Featured Chef, James Beard House Living Legends; Featured Chef, Hotel de Crillion, Paris; and the highly prestigious Restaurant & Institutions Ivy Award. Perhaps the finest hour for the Palace Cafe came when Dickie and his staff served lunch to a president of the United States, the mayor of New Orleans, and a large collection of their friends.

The managing partners of the Palace Cafe are Dickie Brennan, Lauren Brennan Brower, and Steve Pettus, who is not a family member. Pettus, an impressive and knowledgeable man for all seasons, began his career in the restaurant business at age thirteen as a weekend cook at Sizzler Steak House, moved on to Steak and Ale, studied at the University of New Orleans, got a business degree from Millsaps College in Jackson, Mississippi, and a law degree from Loyola. In addition to his work at the Palace Cafe, Pettus serves as an in-house legal counsel for Brennan corporate interests.

Like her big brother Dickie, Lauren Brennan Brower has always had a passion for food and people. And like Dickie, after graduating from LSU, Lauren headed for France. She studied the French language at Ville de Francais and studied cooking at the La Varenne cooking school. Returning to New Orleans, Lauren went to work at Mr. B's, got married, had four children, and is now a managing partner with Dickie and Steve at Palace Cafe and at the new Dickie Brennan's Steakhouse.

I went to Dickie's Steakhouse for the first time with a worldly, well traveled, sophisticated lady friend. We had a drink in the bar and then went down a short flight of stairs to the main dining room. Looking around, she said, "I didn't expect such a warm, inviting atmosphere for ladies in a steakhouse. This is gracious and comfortable. I like it."

Dickie Brennan denies that he started his steakhouse on a whim or dare. He said, "New Orleans is a cosmopolitan town that's known all over the world for great seafood. I had the best steak I've ever had when I lived in Paris. Why not New Orleans?" Dickie Brennan's Steakhouse opened in late fall of 1998 and, from reviews and reports, it's a winner. Here are comments from the April 2000 *Wine Spectator*:

The crew at Palace Cafe and Dickie Brennan's Steakhouse—(left to right) Steve Pettus, Lauren Brennan Brower, and Dickie Brennan. Lauren and Dickie are Dick's children.

Brennan collection

Brennan chefs attending the Grand Chef Festival at Alabama's Grand Hotel at Point Clear. (The Grand Hotel is featured else-where in this book.) Left to right, Jon Michael of BACCO, Michelle McRaney of Mr. B's Bistro, Gus Martin of Palace Cafe, Seth Hargett of the Grand Hotel, James Leeming of Dickie Brennan's Steakhouse, and Laura Karwish of Red Fish Grill.

Brennan collection

You expect the best New Orleans has to offer from the Brennan family, who run the illus-trious Commander's Palace, a *Wine Spectator* Award of Excellence holder, and that's what you're in for at Dickie Brennan's.

Brennan has the physique of a defensive guard for the New Orleans Saints and the face of a choirboy. His southern Louisiana drawl and hearty handshake make you feel real happy you've come.

The subterranean restaurant offers a great bar, side rooms decorated with swords and other martial paraphernalia, as well as a commodious main dining room bustling day and night. . . .

Chef James Leeming gives everything on the menu a Creole twist. . . . The meats are all carefully selected, then—against all conventional wisdom—cooked in a red-hot black-iron skillet, which has the effect of keeping the juices within a well-seared, tasty crust. . . .

Dickie Brennan's Steakhouse is practically next door to the other Brennan restaurants in the area. It's located at 716 Iberville, only one block from Mr. B's and two blocks from Palace Cafe on Canal Street.

RALPH BRENNAN IS A former accountant, and one would not expect him to swing from the romantic side. Yet after he opened BACCO in 1991, the writer Bradley S. O'Leary named the restaurant as one of America's most romantic, and *Zagat Restaurant Guide* followed suit in 1999 by pointing out that BACCO, "thanks to its decor and pampering service, is celebrated as one of New Orleans's top romantic restaurants."

For his part, Ralph says, "BACCO is an Italian restaurant. New Orleanians and Italians alike are drawn to simple, gutsy food with the true taste of superior fresh ingredients. That's what we strive to deliver at BACCO, along with caring service and easy comfort." Always a Brennan, always an innovator, Ralph in 1993 appointed Haley Gabel as executive chef at BACCO, the first female to hold the reins of a Brennan restaurant.

(Ralph's personable and multitalented sister, Lally, spends most of her time at Commander's Palace, where her gifted hand can be found in marketing and public relations.)

BACCO, at 310 Chartres Street in the French Quarter, strives to present a dining alternative in a city where traditional Creole cuisine has always reigned supreme. Toward that end, BACCO features homemade pasta, wood-fired pizzas, fresh regional seafood, and a host of Italian masterpieces highlighted by Crawfish Ravioli. In short, BACCO, with the feel of an Italian *trattoria*, serves up equal parts of classy and casual food in a relaxed atmosphere with a bountiful menu to choose from. BACCO has also caused quite a stir in New Orleans for its "whimsical" design—Venetian chandeliers, Gothic arches, murals, iron gates, wood carvings, and Italian love poems inscribed in the dining booths.

BACCO, from its opening, has constantly captured the attention of the insightful and food-savvy New Orleans *Times-Picayune*, garnering the newspaper's prestigious "four beans" rating for excellence. The paper's "Lagniappe" column stated, "The color scheme, which runs to soft buttery golds and creams, conjures up an earthy palette suggestive of Mediterranean lands."

And applause has come from the national press. *Food & Wine* wrote, "BACCO serves up bracingly fresh Creole-Italian food in soothing sand-colored rooms with gorgeous appointments." *Travel Holiday* said, "Gorgeously appointed rooms evoke images of Italy through the ages . . . a solid hit!" *Bon Appetit* wrote, "With its neoclassic decor and enticing menu, BACCO is a gem." *Where* magazine, New Orleans's prime source for entertainment and dining news, reporting a readers' choice survey for 1999–2000, named it "Best Italian restaurant." And *Southern Living* got right to the point, "Best lovely lunch bargain in the French Quarter."

Ralph Brennan has his versatile hands, fervent imagination, and sterling record in two other innovative dining places in the French Quarter. Both are widely different from BACCO, but equally tantalizing—Red Fish Grill and the Storyville District. The Grill is located at 115 Bourbon Street. Little can be added to the sparkling status and glowing reputation of Red Fish Grill, other than to state the simple fact that *Where*, in its readers' survey, has named this Brennan enterprise "Best Seafood Restaurant in New Orleans" for the last three years in a row.

While BACCO is about food, decor, atmosphere, and romance, and the Red Fish Grill upholds the New Orleans tradition of the best seafood in the world, the Storyville District is essentially about music, New Orleans style. With Storyville, Ralph Brennan teamed up with jazz impresario George Wein and with Quint Davis, producer/director of the New Orleans Jazz & Heritage Festival, to incorporate the best of two New Orleans worlds—superb jazz and fine dining. Moreover, according to Charlee Williamson, Ralph Brennan's marketing director, the Storyville District also seeks to ". . . give the musicians of New Orleans a showcase for their skills, just as Jelly Roll Morton, King Oliver, Sidney Bechet, and Buddy Bolden had in the original Storyville."

ELLA BRENNAN'S DAUGHTER, Ti Martin, is heading the latest Brennan epicurean venture. It's called Foodies Kitchen, a new restaurant and marketing concept that features freshly prepared meals to take out or eat on the premises. Martin told Whit Smyth of *National Restaurant News*, "In 1996, when people for the first time started . . . getting more prepared meals away from home, we figured that [they were] finally voting with their feet, and we started looking for a location." They found a marketplace in Metairie, a suburb of New Orleans. Brennan-Martin said, "[I]t's a very funky and distinctly New Orleans–feeling place . . . Imagine enclosing a farmer's market . . . and . . . combining it with the old New Orleans Solari's."

Alex Brennan-Martin is Ti's older brother and runs the highly successful Brennan's in Houston, which has been a fixture there for decades. Like his sister and cousins, Alex is university-trained (at Tulane) and studied in France at the Institute de Francais and the Ecole de Cuisine La Varenne in Paris. He came to Houston in 1983 and has moved the Brennan standards to notable heights in Texas's largest city. *Gourmet* magazine readers have voted Brennan's in the top three among Houston restaurants, and the *Zagat Survey* stated, "Even New Orleans doesn't have a better New Orleans restaurant."

And the Brennans press on to other venues, other conquests. Last year a Commander's Palace opened in Las Vegas, with Bradford Brennan (Dottie's son) at the helm. It's located in the new Aladdin Hotel across the street from the Bellagio.

In viewing this dynamic scene, Alex Brennan-Martin told *Nation's Restaurant News*, "We're turning some new pages, but not writing a new book. We're doing exciting things, but, hopefully, we're not going to do too much differently than our parents."

I HAVE THE GOOD FORTUNE to know personally many of the members of Brennan's second generation. They have a lot in common, over and above their dedication to the restaurant business, loyalty to the Brennan name, and a strong desire to excel within the Brennan standards. It is noteworthy that, after being trained within the family milieu, with its lofty expectations and high standards, that none have departed the Brennan scene for rosier opportunities with other restaurant groups. True, they have gotten out on their own, in varying degrees, but always under the Brennan banner. All of the juniors are university-trained, mostly with business degrees, and some have studied and worked in other countries, notably France. There is among them a strong competitive spirit, but there seems to be little one-upmanship, jealousy, or petty animosity. In short, they may be ambitious, strong-willed, and aggressive, but above all, they are Brennans and wear the family colors proudly.

Perhaps Ti Brennan-Martin, one of the most vibrant and active members of the Brennan young generation, expressed the family credo best in this note, which appeared in the Fall 2000 issue of *In Command*, the Commander's Palace newsletter:

Only recently did I realize that there was nothing normal about the role food has played in my life. My mother is Ella Brennan. With her brother Dick. her sister Dottie and her late sister Adelaide and brother John they made a formidable team indeed. Much as the U.S. Army Corps of Engineers occasionally succeeds in changing the course of the mighty Mississippi River this determined family of restaurateurs through its involvement with ten restaurants over the last half century has changed the course of New Orleans cooking. For centuries. New Orleans has been known for its rich gastronomic heritage. but little did I know as a child that my mother and uncles and aunts were busy adding a chapter to that story. That story is about the continuing evolution of America's preeminent native cuisine — New Orleans cuisine.

So now, moving into a new century, the Brennan family's beat goes on, in Houston, Las Vegas, and New Orleans . . . always New Orleans.

For more information, contact:

BACCO, 310 Chartres Street in the French Quarter, New Orleans, LA 70130. Phone (504) 522-2426, fax (504) 521-8323. Web site www.bacco.com.

Commander's Palace, 1403 Washington Ave., New Orleans, LA 70130. Phone (504) 899-8221. Web site www.commanderspalace.com.

Dickie Brennan's Steakhouse, 716 Iberville Street, New Orleans, LA 70130. Phone (504) 522-CHOP (2467), fax: (504) 523-0088. Web site www.dbrennanssteakhouse.com.

Foodies Kitchen, at 720 Veterans Boulevard, New Orleans, LA. Web page is www.commanderspalace.com/command2/foodies.html.

Mr. B's Bistro, 201 Royal Street, New Orleans, LA 70130. Phone (504) 523-2078. Web site www.mrbsbistro.com.

Palace Café, 605 Canal Street, New Orleans, LA 70130. Phone (504) 523-1661, fax: (504) 523-1633. Web site www.palacecafe.com.

Red Fish Grill, 115 Bourbon Street, New Orleans, 70130. Phone (504) 598-1200, fax (504) 598-1211. Web site www.redfishgrill.com.

The Storyville District, 125 Bourbon Street, New Orleans, LA 70130. Phone (504) 410-1000. Web site www.thestoryvilledistrict.com.

The National Civil Rights Museum in Memphis
Keeping Dr. King's Movement and Memory Alive

O N APRIL 3, 1968, the night before Rev. Martin Luther King, Jr., was shot and killed, he said in a speech in Memphis, "I don't know what will happen now. We've got some difficult days ahead. But it doesn't matter with me now. Because I've been to the mountaintop—I've seen the promised land. I may not get there with you, but I want you to know tonight that we as a people will get to the promised land."

The next day Dr. King was killed by an assassin's bullet as he stood on the balcony of the Lorraine Motel in downtown Memphis. He was in the city to lead a march in support of striking sanitation workers. Like elsewhere in America, there was rioting and violence in Memphis after the assassination, and the city's recovery was a slow and painful one. But Memphis realized that succeeding generations of Americans should grow up with an understanding of the sacrifices made by their ancestors in the fight for civil rights.

Therefore the National Civil Rights Museum opened in September 1991 and continues to recognize the everyday people who made the movement a turning point in U.S. history. The museum, located in the Lorraine Motel, offers a comprehensive overview of the struggle for civil rights from the mid-1800s to the present, by showing audiovisual exhibits, authentic memorabilia, and scale replicas representing the era. Moreover, it is my impression that the planners of the Museum were seeking to capture the dynamic personality and invincible spirit of Dr. King himself.

An actual cafeteria counter that was the scene of a student sit-in in the 1960s. Sculpted demonstrators still refuse to leave until they are served.

Photo by Starr Smith.

I HAVE SPENT several hours on two different occasions at the museum. Based on my experience as a journalist for NBC Radio covering the civil rights story in the South, it is my opinion that this museum may well be the definitive and acknowledged historical showplace for that far-reaching, epic, magnificent struggle.

My involvement was a long time ago, and visiting the museum was a reminder that I had forgotten a lot about those historic times and meaningful and vivid events. The museum is dramatic and authentic, and it has a sense of theater. It touches the heart in strange and noble ways. It is America's first museum dedicated to documenting and displaying, in an actual setting, the complete history of the movement.

The drama is further enhanced by the fact that you are directly inside the Lorraine Motel, where Dr. King lost his life while carrying on the struggle which, other than the Civil War, has had the most life-changing, essential, and fateful impact on Southern history. I stood on the motel's balcony and looked across to the window where the shots came from. The window is very close; Dr. King didn't have a chance.

As a visitor enters the museum, the balcony where Dr. King died is above and only slightly to the right of the entrance. The cars that Dr. King and his party would have used that fateful night to drive to dinner are parked beneath the balcony.

Just inside the door of the museum is a 7,000 pound sculpture called *Movement to Overcome*, depicting "masses of individuals existing and struggling together," according to Texas artist Michael Pavlovsky, who fashioned the bronze relief.

Nearby is an auditorium where a ten-minute documentary film is shown at regular intervals. This is an audiovisual program of photographs, graphics, lights and sound, and words and music; an orientation film of vivid voltage, keyed to the realistic and gripping exhibits on display just outside the door.

Each exhibit is designed to further the understanding of the history, the people, and the struggle of this movement that touched every facet of American society. Introductory exhibits depict the African American struggle in this country up to the mid-1950s. While the major focus of the museum spans the period from 1954 through the

National Civil Rights Museum at the Lorraine Motel, where Rev. Martin Luther King, Jr., was assassinated April 4, 1968. The second-floor room with open drapes was his. The cars to be used that night remain where they were parked when he was shot.

Photo by Starr Smith.

161

America's loss is memorialized by this plaque outside King's room. Ralph Abernathy succeeded King as the leader of the civil rights movement.

Photo by Starr Smith.

MARTIN LUTHER KING, JR.
JAN. 15, 1929 —— APR. 4, 1968
FOUNDING PRESIDENT
SOUTHERN CHRISTIAN LEADERSHIP CONFERENCE
"THEY SAID ONE TO ANOTHER,
BEHOLD, HERE COMETH THE DREAMER...
LET US SLAY HIM...
AND WE SHALL SEE WHAT WILL BECOME OF HIS DREAM
GENESIS 37: 19-20
RALPH DAVID ABERNATHY, PRESIDENT

death of Dr. King, the roots of the movement go back much further, and these early efforts are also covered.

Highlighting the museum are fifteen primary exhibits, including:

Brown vs. Board of Education—The landmark 1954 decision by the U.S. Supreme Court that struck down the "separate but equal" doctrine in American's public schools.

The Montgomery Bus Boycott—The boycott, precipitated by the arrest of Rosa Parks, and which is considered the beginning of the modern civil rights movement, is symbolized by a real Montgomery city bus from that era.

Little Rock's Central High School—Depicts the confrontation that unfolded over the rights of nine black students to enroll. President Eisenhower sent in federal troops to protect the students and enforce the law.

The Student Sit-In Movement—One of the museum's most dramatic scenes: an actual counter where a sit-in occurred, with statues of the students involved.

The Freedom Riders—Features a burned-out Greyhound bus like the ones used in the 1961 Freedom Rides. The buses were sometimes stopped and burned by racists.

The Battle for Ole Miss—Commemorates the protests and the riot precipitated by the admission of James Meredith, the first black student at the University of Mississippi. Two people were killed by rioters.

The March on Washington—Depicts Dr. King's legendary "I Have a Dream" speech. The march is considered by many to be the movement's crowning moment.

The Selma to Montgomery March—Features a replica of the Edmund Pettus Bridge, where marchers were beaten by law enforcement officers.

The interior of King's room has been left just as it was when he was shot.

Photo by Starr Smith.

The Life of Dr. King—A biographical exhibit explores King's philosophies and his career.

Dr. King's Death—The balcony where Dr. King was shot, outside rooms 306 and 307 of the Lorraine Motel. These two rooms can be viewed just as they were when he died, and, of course, they are the emotional focus of the museum.

The Struggle Continues—An epilogue that encourages visitors to remember that the movement is an ongoing, contemporary battle, and there is much work left to be done.

AT THE OPENING of the museum ten years ago, Judge D'Army Bailey of Memphis, one of the founders of the museum and chairman of the National Civil Rights Museum Foundation, said, "To older generations, I think the museum will serve as a national center of remembrance for those who helped, who suffered, and who struggle still. For young people, I hope it will provide the inspiration to pursue the many opportunities that emerged from the struggle."

Now, millions of visitors later, the vision of the museum's creators has turned into tangible reality and a soaring tribute to Dr. King's dream. The *New York Times* stated, "The museum [holds] the first comprehensive exhibit documenting the civil rights movement in this country." The *Atlanta Journal-Constitution* said that the museum "shouldn't be remembered as the place where Dr. King died. It should be remembered as the place where the dream is being kept alive."

For more information, contact the National Civil Rights Museum, 450 Mulberry St., Memphis, TN 38103-4214. Phone (901) 521-9699. Web site www.midsouth.rr.com/civilrights.

Delta Air Lines
The South's Window to the World

I
N THE SUMMER and early fall of the year 2000, Southern skywatchers were somewhat surprised to see a graceful silver twin-engine prop-driven airplane gracing the skies over Atlanta, Tallahassee, Montgomery, Pensacola, and other cities in the region. The splendid old plane, of another time, cruised majestically along through the blue-white summer sky, its props developing a sedate and impassive air speed of 170 miles per hour. It carried the bold and familiar blue and white signature of Delta Air Lines.

The plane was Ship 41, the first DC-3 to join the fledgling Delta fleet in 1940, now carefully and fondly restored by scores of Delta volunteers in Atlanta and flown by retired Delta captains. Ship 41 was making a series of goodwill visits to Delta cities.

I had the opportunity to inspect Ship 41 and hear its remarkable history from Captain Sam Bass, the pilot, and James Ray, the restoration expert who had guided the renovation of the grand old plane and given it a glamorous new life in the modern world. The noble task that brought Ship 41 to its second life began more than ten years ago. A group of retired Delta captains launched a Herculean task to find the first Douglas DC-3 to be delivered to Delta's then new headquarters in Atlanta, after moving from Monroe, Louisiana. That move placed Delta in direct competition with the stronger Eastern Airlines. Delta eventually won that battle, so therefore an original and restored DC-3 would salute not only the gallant plane, but also the thousands of loyal and intrepid employees who helped Delta survive competitive and difficult times and move on to become one of the world's great airlines.

Moreover, other goals were involved: to set an unprecedented standard in DC-3 restoration and to create a technical work of art that would fly and thrill employees, customers, children, aviation aficionados, and visitors. For his part, Leo Mullin, chairman of Delta, has said, "This beautiful aircraft represents the combined efforts of many Delta people, both active and retired, who want to represent Delta's heritage of service and quality. They have accomplished their goals. Ship 41 clearly demonstrates the Delta tradition of courtesy, graciousness, and customer attention."

Ship 41 was the first DC-3 placed into Delta's passenger schedule, entering service on Christmas Eve, 1940. Over the years, Delta had a total of twenty-three DC-3s. These aircraft served Delta until 1963.

The dramatic quest and labor of love to find the first Delta DC-3, after crestfallen and disappointing times, reached a happy fruition in the sunny Caribbean, where the

Ship 41, Delta's first DC-3, now totally refurbished and returned to 1940s condition, seen here on a goodwill mission to one of Delta's Southern cities.

Photo by Starr Smith.

plane, then flying cargo, was located. Thus on March 26, 1993, after fifty-three years in commercial aviation, and eleven owners after Delta, Ship 41 lifted off from San Juan, Puerto Rico, bound for Atlanta, with a Delta jet captain and a retired Delta captain at the controls.

THE PLANE WAS PARKED in a Delta hangar for nearly two years before reconstruction work began. Ship 41's long and active life—78,000 hours flying time—had taken its toll. Beginning in 1995, hundreds of volunteers, active and retired mechanics, pilots, other Delta employees and family members, working with restoration manager James Ray, set about their arduous but loving task to return Ship 41 to its former glory. When finished, the ship would embark on a theatrical career and become an on-stage, on-display personality.

Few DC-3s had flown in passenger service since the mid-1960s, so every part had to located, refurbished, or entirely replicated. For example, a rare matching set of twenty-one passenger seats was found in a barn in Jackson, Mississippi. Although the 134 parts in each seat had to be reconditioned, the search team was overjoyed to find them. The plane was completely renovated from nose to tail, frequently requiring the craftsmanship of mechanics to fabricate parts that no longer existed. The twin-engine DC-3 was painstakingly restored to better-than-new condition, from the polished aluminum exterior to the leather and fabric interior, highlighted by new window curtains and polished stainless steel fixtures throughout the cabin.

Altogether the restoration of Ship 41 took almost ten years of dedication and hard work from hundreds of individuals and several organizations. The top volunteers donated from 40 to 1000 hours of time and effort on the project. Finally they all watched on November 17, 1999, as Delta Chairman Mullin and Birdie Bomar, who was a stewardess on Ship 41's maiden and retirement flights, christened the valiant old air warrior, and they all cheered as the plane roared down the runway at Atlanta's Hartsfield International Airport. Since then Ship 41 has won two prestigious awards: the Georgia Trust for Historic Preservation's 2000 Outstanding Achievement Award and a gold Lindy-Special Award–Judges' Choice trophy at the international 2000 air show in Oshkosh, Wisconsin. Paulette O'Donnell, manager of the Delta Heritage Museum at Delta headquarters in

Atlanta, tells me that plans are moving forward for an extension of the museum and a hangar for Ship 41, where it can be viewed by the public in all of its majestic splendor.

Shortly after my encounter with Ship 41, I flew out of Atlanta on Delta for Madrid, Spain. Earlier that year, I had flown on Delta's inaugural flight to South Africa. Before takeoff on both flights, looking out the windows of the giant transoceanic jets, I observed literally scores of Delta planes parked at passenger gates of Hartsfield International Airport. Delta has 906 flights departing from Atlanta every day. Of these, 43 are international flights—direct from Atlanta—to Amsterdam, Brussels, Cape Town, Dublin, Frankfurt, London, Mexico City, Paris, Rome, Sao Paulo, Tokyo, Toronto, Zurich, and many other world destinations. There are daily Delta flights from Atlanta to Latin and South America—Aruba, Costa Rica, El Salvador, Guatemala, Panama, Peru, Venezuela, and, added late in 2000, Chile and Argentina.

Indeed, Delta has established an aerial global link from Atlanta—the South's Window to the World.

IN 1919 THE LITTLE Alabama town of Enterprise erected a monument to the boll weevil after that pest demolished most of the area's cotton crops, forcing Coffee County farmers to diversify into other crops like peanuts, corn, hay, and sugar cane. There's also a boll weevil in Delta's past. The powerful little insect had a primal role in the early life and history of the great airline.

The time was the early 1920s. The place was the cotton-growing area around Monroe and Tallulah, Louisiana. The problem was the boll weevil, which had come to the South from Mexico around the turn of the century, and was devastating the cotton fields. Enter a young agriculture agent working for the Extension Department of Louisiana State University, who was also an aviation enthusiast. His name was Collett Everman (C. E.) Woolman, an agricultural engineering graduate of the University of Illinois. The boll weevil scourge had become such a severe economic threat to the area that the U.S. government established a laboratory in Tallulah for an intensified extermination project.

The laboratory was directed by Dr. B. R. Coad; Woolman was his assistant. First the team had to develop a chemical to kill the boll weevil in large numbers, and second they had to devise a method of application that was faster and more effective than hand-

C. E. Woolman, Delta founder, chairman, and CEO until his death on September 11, 1966.

Photo courtesy of Delta Air Lines.

TravelAir S-6000B, one of four of its kind that made up Delta Air Service's entire fleet in 1929. The plane carried five passengers, cruised at 100 mph, and had a maximum range of 500 miles.

Photo by Starr Smith.

sprinkling. The two young pioneers had a chemical that would stop the boll weevil—lead arsenate. With the help of a small Congressional appropriation and two Army-furnished planes called Jennies, they experimented with, and perfected, a new technique of application—a delivery system called cotton dusting.

Good things continued to fall into place. In 1923 a New York airplane manufacturer made a forced landing in Tallulah due to engine trouble. The New York entrepreneur was George Post, a man well tuned in to the times. Post spent enough time in Tallulah, while his plane was being serviced, to discover and become enthusiastic about aerial crop dusting. The next year he formed a separate division of his company, called

Huff Daland Dusters. In the spring of 1925, C. E. Woolman combined his entomological-agricultural work with his first love—aviation—and joined Huff Daland Dusters, which was headquartered in nearby Monroe. It was a major and successful career move for Woolman. He brought to the new company integrity, a genial personality, a propensity for hard work, and a stubborn resistance to failure.

Woolman did not fail. On his watch, Huff Daland built the first planes specifically designed for dusting, and in due course the company became the largest privately

ta flight line at Atlanta Hartsfield International Airport, representing only a small portion of Delta's 765-plane fleet.

Photo courtesy of Delta Air Lines.

Delta General Office at Monroe, Louisiana, ca. 1929–30.
Photo courtesy of Delta Air Lines.

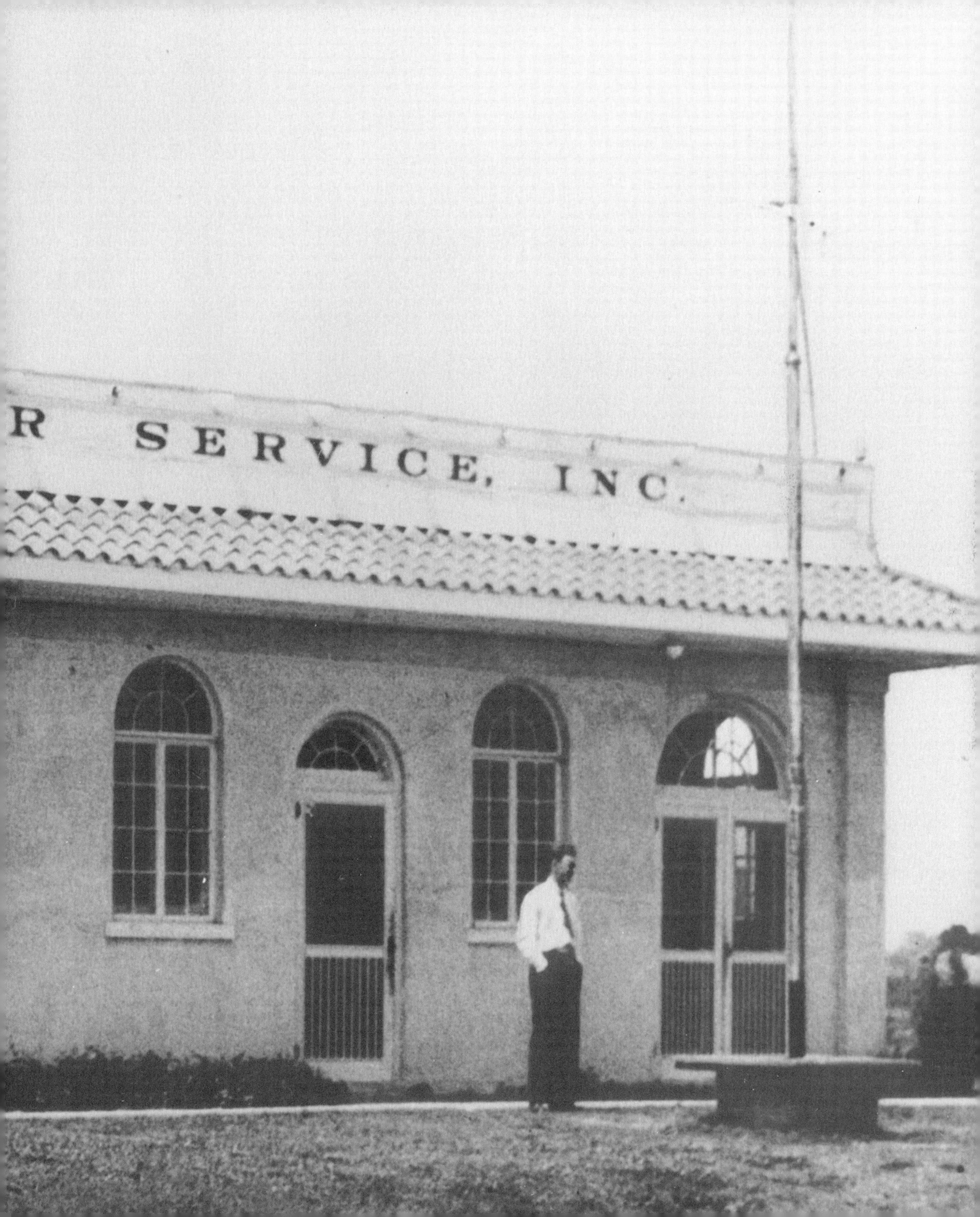
R SERVICE, INC.

Leo Mullin, current Delta chairman and CEO.

owned aircraft fleet in the world, with twenty-five planes. Since the dusting company operated only in the summer months, Woolman decided to move his planes, during nonproductive times, southward to Peru where the seasons are reversed. That way they earned money year-round. This move proved to be extremely serendipitous, for it was in Peru that Woolman first visualized the possibility of passenger service by air. (It is noteworthy that, as the twentieth century was drawing to a close, Delta, the airline that Woolman founded, inaugurated direct nonstop flights from Atlanta, the headquarters he later established, to Peru, where his vision was first realized.)

Lady Luck flew with Woolman from Peru back to Monroe in 1928. He discovered that George Post was interested in selling the crop dusting company. Moving with dispatch, he quickly rounded up a group of Monroe investors and they purchased the Huff Daland equipment. Forthwith the company's name was changed to Delta Air Service, for the Mississippi Delta, and the new group, in high spirits, purchased four 5-passenger, 90-mile-per-hour Travel Air monoplanes.

WHILE DELTA WAS BUSY developing its Southern routes, three other airlines—each destined to play key roles in Delta's future—were flying high and moving forward, two in the West and one in the Northeast. Chicago and Southern Air Lines (C&S) became part of Delta through a merger in 1953. Northeast Airlines merged with Delta in 1972, and Western Air Lines was merged into Delta in 1987. These mergers added revenue-producing routes, tremendous corporate strength, and national prestige to Delta, and greatly increased its prominence in the American air transportation community. Delta quickly became a leader in new jet models among the world's airlines, introducing the DC-8 in 1959, the CV-880 in 1960, and the DC-9 in 1965.

Delta's route system expanded to a greater extent in the 1970s, not only through the mergers, but also through a number of routes awarded by the Civil Aeronautics Board. Delta's first transatlantic route was inaugurated on April 30, 1978, from Atlanta to London. The Airline Deregulation Act of 1978 brought more changes, virtually overnight, than had been experienced in the entire forty years that airlines had been under formal government regulation. Yet under steady, progressive, and adroit management—first under the redoubtable Woolman and later under a series of his successors—Delta flew on toward its destiny as one of the world's great airlines.

Some highlights in the brilliant history of this remarkable Southern company:

In 1958, with the help of a Delta flight attendant, Mrs. Hugh Ector gave birth to a daughter while in mid-flight, at 9,000 feet, over Malden, Missouri. Delta "wings" (uniform adornments) were used as diaper pins.

In 1982, in a high-spirited display of loyalty and confidence, Delta employees purchased a $30 million Boeing 767. It was paid for by payroll deductions and was called *The Spirit of Delta*.

In 1991, in a pivotal and far-reaching move, Delta purchased essentially all of Pan Am's transatlantic flight authorities. It was the largest acquisition of flights in airline history, making Delta a global carrier.

In 1992 Delta received the Rex Award from readers of *ASTA Agency Management*, a publication for travel agents. In 1993 the airline received a second Rex award, along with a *Zagat Survey* Travel Excellence Award.

In 1995, Delta was named Best Airline by the *Robb Report*. It received the J. D. Power Award as best among major carriers for long-haul and short-haul flights.

Delta was named the official airline of the 1996 Atlanta Centennial Olympic Games. Delta unveiled the *Centennial Spirit*, a new jet brilliantly painted in an Olympic design, that flew the Olympic flame from Athens, Greece, to Los Angeles, from where it was carried across the country for the games.

And 1999 was a banner year. *Air Transport* magazine named Delta as Airline of the Year. Delta was named Best Managed Major Airline by *Aviation Week and Space Technology* magazine. The Federal Aviation Administration presented Delta with the Diamond Award in its Aviation Maintenance Technician Safety Award Program. And, perhaps the highest honor, 105 million passengers traveled on Delta that year.

Delta is the largest U.S. domestic carrier, with 105.4 million enplanements in 1999, followed by United with 86.5 million. Delta was the only major network carrier to be ranked in the top three in the major passenger-service categories: third highest in on-time arrivals, second lowest in mishandled baggage, and lowest in consumer complaints.

Delta's jet fleet totals 765 aircraft, including regional jets. Taking off on 5,370 daily flights, the airline flies to 352 cities, including Delta, Delta-connection, and other flights. From Atlanta, Delta has 906 daily departures, including commuter flights, serving 163 cities.

There are four U.S. hubs: Atlanta, Cincinnati, Dallas/Fort Worth, and Salt Lake City. The major Delta gateway cities are Atlanta for Europe and South and Central America; Portland, Oregon, for the Pacific area; and New York (JFK) for Europe and points beyond. A Delta jet takes off somewhere in the world every thirty-three seconds.

IN SHORT, IN LESS than seventy-five years, this Southern-born airline has advanced, from a small local operation with a handful of employees serving a single route, to one of the largest airlines in the world, flying an ultramodern jet fleet to destinations around the globe, and carrying more passengers than any airline in the world—117 million in 2000.

In 1997, Leo Mullin became Delta's chairman and CEO. Mullin, who has earned three degrees from Harvard, had served with some of America's most prestigious firms before joining Delta, including First Chicago Bank, Conrail, and Commonwealth Edison. A thinker and visionary as well as a crack businessman, Mullin was quoted in the January 2001 issue of *Vanity Fair* (commenting on Stephen Ambrose's book *Nothing Like It in the World: The Men Who Built the Transcontinental Railroad 1865–1869*), "Ambrose's book sparked an aviation thought: we have to harness that same pioneering vision to support our nation's growing demand for air travel. A progressive vision prevailed then; a progressive vision should prevail now."

For more information, visit web site www.delta.com.

The Grove Park Inn in Asheville
Luxury and Tradition in the Mountains

IN THE EARLY YEARS of this century, a visionary by the name of Edwin Grove came to the little North Carolina mountain town of Asheville from his home in St. Louis. He had come to Asheville on summer holiday and found the mountain air so cool and invigorating that he decided to build a hotel there. This was not to be just an ordinary place for drummers and occasional tourists, but was to be "built not for the present alone, but for ages to come, and the admiration of generations yet unborn." This was an ambitious order, but Mr. Grove was not an ordinary man; he planned big. He headed a company in St. Louis that made and sold the vastly successful Grove's Tasteless Chill Tonic. The vision of constructing the hotel was just another challenge to the new resident of Asheville's Blue Ridge Mountains.

Mr. Grove laid his plans in the summer of 1912 and the hotel opened on July 12, 1913, less than a year later. Naturally, the new resort was called the Grove Park Inn. Making the official dedication address was another man who knew a thing or two about the pursuit of dreams—William Jennings Bryan, the famed lawyer and politician.

Earlier, when Mr. Grove had first visualized his unique hotel overlooking the mountains, he could not find an architect to his liking. So in the manner of willful and wealthy men, he had commandeered his son-in-law, a newspaperman named Fred Seely. Using giant boulders from Sunset Mountain, hauled to the site by mule-drawn wagons and set in place by Italian artisans and Asheville laborers, Mr. Seely and Mr. Grove built a hotel that has since become known as one of the finest resort hotels in the world.

The Great Hall (or lobby) of the Inn. Note the large fireplace at the far end.

Fred Seely managed the inn until 1927. He was another man of strong will and positive views. His rules at the inn were strict: pets forbidden, slamming of doors not allowed, children discouraged, and only low tones and whispers allowed after 10:30 P.M. His stated objective was "to maintain a place where tired, busy people may get away from all annoyances and rest their nerves." Mr. Seely's guests apparently liked his policy.

Thus the hotel stands today, an American institution approaching its first hundred years, and enrolled in the National Register of Historical Places in 1973. The Grove Park Inn is not only historical, but is really first-rate, taking its place along with the Homestead,

One of the two large fireplaces in the Great Hall (main lobby). Each fireplace burns twelve-foot logs.

Prominent guests during the Inn's early years: (left to right) Harvey Firestone, Sr., Thomas Edison, Harvey Firestone, Jr., Horatio Seymour, Henry Ford, and hotel manager Fred Seely.

the Greenbrier, and Point Clear's Grand Hotel in the roll call of America's premier resort hotels.

On the early guest registers are the names of Thomas Edison, Harvey Firestone, Henry Ford, President Woodrow Wilson, and President Franklin D. Roosevelt. General Dwight Eisenhower stayed at the Inn. The legendary composer Bela Bartok, fleeing tyranny in Europe, came to the Inn in 1944 and worked on his Concerto No. 3 for Piano and Orchestra. There is a suite named for F. Scott Fitzgerald, who stayed there on his visits to his wife Zelda's sanitarium nearby. It is said that he did some writing there, probably his *Saturday Evening Post* short stories.

I reside in Montgomery, which was Zelda's hometown. I have oftentimes, in summer, sat with drink in hand on the terrace of the Grove Park Inn, watching the sun set and darkness come to the faraway mountains, thinking of the visits that Fitzgerald made to Zelda when she was in the hospital nearby, and imagining the quiet dinners they may have had at the Inn.

THE GROVE PARK LOBBY is called the Great Hall. It is 120 feet long and 80 feet wide, anchored at each end by massive fireplaces large enough to burn twelve-foot logs. Since the Inn was originally built as a winter resort, these great fireplaces became the talk of America and beyond. Even now they are attention-getters, especially around Christmas and New Year's, with a blazing fire centered at each end of the Great Hall.

When the Inn was built, a huge orchestral organ with seven thousand pipes was constructed and installed in the Great Hall, and concerts were held nightly for guests.

The Inn is now open year-round and has proven as popular in summer as in winter. In 1976 the Country Club of Asheville, with its 18-hole golf course, was purchased to become part of the hotel complex, and was remodeled in 1985. The Inn has a total of 510 guest rooms, including the Main Building (the Inn) and two wings, the Sammons and the Vanderbilt, added in 1984 and 1988.

The resort sits on 140 acres atop Sunset Mountain in the heart of the Blue Ridge range. It is two miles from downtown Asheville on Macon Avenue.

Main building of the Inn is made of native boulders from North Carolina mountains. The Inn was finished in 1913; William Jennings Bryan made the official opening address. Two wings (not shown) have been added in recent years, bringing the total number of rooms to 510.

Photo by Starr Smith.

Like all celebrated resorts, the Inn leaves no stone unturned to please its customers. It has everything. When a guest arrives, the Inn sees no reason for him or her to leave the premises for any reason. The three main dining rooms, the Blue Ridge, Terrace, and Carolina Cafe, and, in season, the Cabana and Sunset Terrace, offer the best food in the area. I especially like the Sunset Terrace for both lunch and dinner. The Great Hall Lobby Bar, with the fire going, is the place for drinks in winter, and, just outside, the Terrace is fine in summer.

In World War II the Grove Park Inn had one of the most intriguing missions of any resort in America. The U.S. government leased it, and in 1942 Axis diplomats lived there while awaiting repatriation to their own countries. The Inn's history states that they were treated as ordinary guests and paid their own expenses. Later in the War, the Inn served both the Navy and Army as a rest center for servicemen and women.

After the War, the Inn passed through several owners until, happily, in 1955 it was purchased by a Texan, Charles Sammons of Dallas, thereby returning the Inn to individual ownership that remains today. Mr. Sammons is no longer alive, but his widow, Elaine, owns the Inn and resides there in her own suites for parts of every year while she keeps a lively eye on all activities.

As one who knows the Grove Park Inn, I can say that any visit is memorable. But the really big occasions are the Thanksgiving House Party, a Grove Park Inn Christmas, and the New Year's Eve Celebration. Perhaps these times are ultraspecial because the magnificent fires are roaring in the twin fireplaces of the Great Hall.

For more information: Grove Park Inn and Country Club, 290 Macon Avenue, Asheville, NC 28804. Reservations (800) 438-5800, phone (828) 252-2711, fax (828) 253-7053. Web site www.groveparkinn.com.

The Mighty Eighth Air Force Heritage Museum
Remembering the Brave Airmen of World War II

SHORTLY AFTER PEARL Harbor, the "officials at the highest levels of the United States and British governments, and their military advisers, determined that the major United States effort to save Europe would be through heavy bombardment of the German heartland," according to an Eighth Air Force history at the Mighty Eighth Air Force Heritage Museum near Savannah, Georgia.

The history continues, "With that mission in mind, the Eighth Air Force was formed and began operations in 1942. The Eighth became the largest air force in aviation history. The cost in casualties of the brave young men, who were never turned back by enemy action, was awesome. Of an estimated 200,000 combat-crew personnel, 26,000 were killed, 28,000 became prisoners of war, and 9,000 bombers were shot down by enemy fire. With the inclusion of the ground crews, 350,000 Americans served with the Eighth during World War II in England."

The first commander of the Eighth Air Force was Gen. Ira Eaker, who, along with Gens. Henry "Hap" Arnold and Carl Spaatz, was already a legend in American military aviation.

When Gen. Eaker and the Eighth Air Force arrived in England in early 1942, the Royal Air Force Bomber Command, led by the redoubtable Arthur "Bomber" Harris, had been flying missions against Nazi Germany since 1939. Soon after Eaker began to lead the Eighth in combat. He made a speech in London to veteran RAF officers and ranking civilians, all of whom had been heavily engaged in the war effort. He said, "I'm not going to

African-Americans in Aviation

The Tuskegee Airmen

We were all in it together—a touching exhibit honoring the heroics of the famous Tuskegee Airmen in WWII.

The museum's busts of the legendary Gen. Jim Doolittle (left) and Gen. Ira Eaker, who was the Eighth's first commander.

A fighter swoops and a bomber climbs over one of the museum's many gripping exhibits.

The valor, deeds, and memories of the men and women of the Eighth Air Force have been enshrined in this modern museum near Savannah, where the Eighth was born.

Lt. Gen. E. C. "Buck" Shuler (Ret.), one of the museum's founders, with the bust of Jimmy Stewart. Shuler is a former peacetime commander of the Eighth. Stewart served in the Eighth during WW II.

All photos on these two pages by Starr Smith.

do much talking until the Eighth Air Force has done some fighting. But when we leave, I hope you'll be glad we came."

The wings are yellow, the fuselage blue, the propeller white with red tips. One of many beautiful and historic planes at the museum.

Photo by Starr Smith.

Three years later, when the Germans were defeated, the Eighth Air Force had become the mightiest and most successful air-war machine in the history of military combat. Working in concert with RAF Bomber Command, which bombed German targets at night, the Eighth, flying four-engine B-17s and B-24s in precision bombing patterns in the daytime, led the way to victory.

NOW, AFTER MORE THAN fifty years, the valor, deeds, exploits, adventures, and memories of the men and women of the Eighth Air Force, and those unforgettable days and nights in wartime England, have been enshrined in a museum near the same historic Southern town where the Eighth was born, Savannah, Georgia.

Low-tech weapons of war—a Jeep and a bicycle, common sights around air bases in wartime England.

Photo by Starr Smith.

I had the high honor and extreme good fortune to fly with the Eighth Air Force in those momentous war years in England, as a combat intelligence officer posted with the 453rd Bomb Group, a B-24 outfit stationed near Cambridge in East Anglia. Not long ago, on a gray Saturday, I spent a few hours of muted excitement and somber reflection at the museum.

The museum opened in 1996, and since that time a million visitors, many of them Eighth Air Force veterans, have come to the modern state-of-the-art building.

The huge Eighth Air Force insignia is inlaid into the floor of the rotunda. Banners that fly overhead represent every bomber, fighter group, and wing of the Eighth, and plaques detail every unit. Some of the treasures include a World War II jeep and an

English bicycle like the one I used to ride around the bomber base. A Schweinfurt-Regensburg exhibit showcases flight artifacts. There is also a detailed diorama of an American bomber base in England, and a Nissen hut, so like the one I entered on many a cold morning to brief the flight crews before they left on that day's mission. The museum's art gallery features a bust of Eaker and Gen. Jimmy Doolittle, another Eighth Air Force commander, and a long wall has photographs of Eighth Air Force heroes who won the Congressional Medal of Honor, including many Southerners.

The decision to place the museum near Savannah was both symbolic and sentimental. The Eighth was formed there on Bull Street. After moving to England, the headquarters was at a girls school at High Wycombe, near London. At full strength during the war, the Eighth consisted of 65 heavy-bomber groups, 20 fighter groups, 3 air divisions, 4 headquarters, and supply, maintenance, and repair depots, scattered throughout the United Kingdom, all of which are represented in the museum.

The Eighth is still an active part of the U.S. military establishment. The museum's chairman, Lt. Gen. E. G. "Buck" Shuler of Alexander City, Alabama, says, "The Heritage Museum was built to honor the more than one million men and women who have served in the Eighth, in war and peace, since it was created in 1942." Shuler, now retired, is a former commander of the peacetime Eighth.

Perhaps the museum's major attraction is a large exhibit area that is linked by a story line that takes visitors from pre–World War II days right up to the present-day Eighth Air Force and its current assignments. Three main theaters tell the story: Freedom, Mission Experience, and the Battle of Britain.

I was deeply moved by the prisoner of war, escape, and evasion exhibits. Equally dramatic and moving was the Memorial Garden with its Wall of Valor, which already has more than four hundred plaques honoring Eighth Air Force veterans and crews.

Suspended from the ceiling of the museum's largest exhibition hall is a P-51 Mustang fighter aircraft, the type of plane that the bomber crews called their "little friend" on fighter-escorted bombing missions deep into Germany. Placed beneath the Mustang is a German fighter plane, which is distinctive because it is a jet. Jet planes only came into action very late in the war.

In his definitive book on the air war in Europe, *To Command the Sky*, the Southern writer Wesley Newton gives high praise to Maj. Gen. Fred Anderson, commander of the

Eighth Air Force Bomber Command. Gen. Anderson's uniforms are on display at the museum.

MANY FAMOUS PEOPLE served in the Eighth. Jimmy Stewart, the Hollywood actor, was a B-24 Liberator combat pilot, group operations officer, and, at war's end, a wing commander. He flew twenty combat missions with the Eighth. Actor Clark Gable flew missions as a gunner in the Eighth, and Walter Matthau, also to become a movie star, was a sergeant. Col. Beirne Lay, author of *Twelve O'clock High*, and Paul Tibbetts, commander of the Enola Gay, the plane that dropped the first atomic bomb, got their first taste of combat when they flew the Eighth's first mission. There is a bronze bust of Jimmy Stewart in the museum, along with Gens. Doolittle, Spaatz, and Eaker.

The renowned Washington lawyer Ramsay Potts, a retired Reserve major general, who was a flight leader on the heroic Ploesti raid early in the war, was an Eighth Air Force B-24 group commander, and now serves on the museum's board of directors. Potts is from Memphis and is a graduate of the University of North Carolina.

Haynes Thompson of Montgomery, a former United Press International foreign correspondent who was an Air Force officer in England and France in World War II, remembers that his friend Walter Cronkite, who was then a United Press war correspondent, flew several missions over Germany with the Eighth. Cronkite, who later went on to worldwide fame as a CBS newsman, has visited the museum. He said, "The museum is an important history lesson that is taught in the best possible fashion. . . . these displays take you from the prewar days of the Nazi aggression right on through to the defeat of the Third Reich, and the Eighth Air Force's obvious major contribution to gaining the victory."

The museum is located near Savannah at exit 102 (formerly exit 18) off Interstate 95, just north of Interstate 16. It is open seven days a week from 9 A.M. to 6 P.M. There is an admission charge. For information, contact the Mighty Eighth Air Force Heritage Museum, PO Box 1992, Savannah, GA 31402. Phone (912) 748-8888 or fax (912) 748-0209. Web site www.mighty8thmuseum.com.

Ave Maria Grotto

Brother Joe's Miniature Religious Wonders

BROTHER JOSEPH ZOETTI was born in Bavaria in 1878. He was small, modest, and shy, and liked to work with his hands. He came to America to follow his dream of becoming a Catholic monk. So it was that the year 1892 found the young Bavarian at the new St. Bernard Abbey in the wooded, rolling hills just outside Cullman, in north Alabama. Brother Joe, as he was known in the Abbey, went on to become a member of the Benedictine Order.

From the time of his arrival at St. Bernard until his death in 1961, he seldom ventured far from the peace and solitude of the Abbey. His days and nights, like those of his brothers in the Order, were spent in prayer, study, meditation, and the labor of maintaining a school, the grounds, a farm, and a cattle ranch, all run in the fast-growing 800-acre compound. This was in keeping with the dictum of "Work and Pray."

Thus it was the lot of Brother Joe to shovel coal and to man the furnace in the boiler room that provided power for the Abbey. Later a construction accident left him a hunchback. The injury did not stop Brother Joe. In 1897 his dream was realized. He was installed as a monk in the St. Benedictine order at St. Bernard Abbey. His work in the power plant went on as before.

But his life's work and ultimate destiny were not in the boiler room. There was more—a hidden talent. The surging spirit, creative desire, artistic ingenuity, and vivid imagination of the shy and gentle monk found an innovative and inspired avenue in his gifted hands.

Brother Joe's miniature of St. Peter's Basilica in Rome.

Today Brother Joseph Zoetti's life work, legacy, and gift to the world is the Ave Maria Grotto at St. Bernard, an incomparable collection of miniature replicas of meaningful religious structures and significant historical buildings from around the world.

This is the "Small World of Brother Joe." To this miniature domain, close by a little town in Alabama, come every year 75,000 visitors from all points on the globe. Many say that this humble creation by the little monk has given inspiration and hope to countless numbers of people. The Grotto, in a tree-shaded glen of four acres on the site of an old stone quarry on the Abbey grounds, has become a leading tourist attraction in the South.

Perhaps the crowning stroke is Brother Joe's Basilica of Lourdes, France. This miniature building with its gothic tower measures about three feet tall; the actual tower is 230 feet. It is notable that the Lourdes Basilica masterpiece was completed in 1958, only three years before Brother Joe died in 1961 at the age of eighty-three.

LIKE BROTHER JOE himself, the beginning of the Grotto was modest in scope. In those early days he collected old bricks, glass, metal, marbles, stone, pieces of pipe, bottles,

Brother Joe worked for fifty years to create his miniature masterpieces. He died at 83 after spending most of his life at St. Bernard Abbey.

196

Brother Joe's miniature of the Basilica in Lourdes, France.

cups, and household items. A room near the power plant was converted into a workshop. He studied photos, postcards, books, magazines, and brochures, many provided by helpful friends. Experimenting with cement, he fashioned his meager materials into his little kingdom.

His most amazing talent was the ability to study a picture of a building and construct it with such skill that the finished product was almost identical. He was an avid reader and studied even the most minute structural details of his buildings. Although there are about 125 miniatures at the Grotto, Brother Joe saw, in person, only six of the places that he created.

At first Brother Joe's remarkable miniatures were viewed only by his fellow monks. But soon the word spread. As a result, the Abbey built a special place for prayer and religious services and a tour of Brother Joe's work. It was named the Ave Maria Grotto, and in 1934 was dedicated and opened to an admiring public.

In the center of the display is the actual place of worship, with a marble altar, statues, and figures carrying out the religious motif. The tour begins in the gift shop and follows a loose circle. But the crowds come to see Brother Joe's handiwork in the secluded statuary garden. A winding, scenic pathway down a sloping hill leads to the exhibit, which is artistically and dramatically arranged.

There is the Holy Land, with the Temple of Jerusalem, Herod's Gate, Gethsemane, and other biblical scenes. Brother Joe made the huge dome of St. Peter's Basilica in Rome from a bird cage. In Rome, the real dome stands over the tomb of the apostle Peter, the first Pope, and the basilica covers four acres and holds seventy thousand people. But Brother Joe's detailed miniature of the famous church is startling.

So too are the Monte Cassino Abbey in Italy, the Pantheon, St. Scholastica of Subiaco near Rome, the Leaning Tower of Pisa, the Colosseum, the Appius Claudius Aqueduct, Bethlehem Cave, the shrine of Our Lady of Guadelupe, the Benedictine monastery in Korea, the Fortress of Antonia, the Resurrection, the Ten Commandments, the Tomb of Lazarus, the Hanging Gardens of Babylon, the pyramids, the Brazen Serpent, and many other miniatures depicting religious themes.

Some of the most touching are Castle Trausnitz and St. Martin's church, miniatures of actual buildings in Brother Joe's birthplace of Landshut, Bavaria, which he constructed from memory.

HIGHLY PATRIOTIC AND deeply devoted to his adopted land, Brother Joe fashioned many famous landmarks of America in his display. There are miniatures of the Statue of Liberty; the Alamo; the Round Tower, a mysterious stone structure in Rhode Island thought to have been built by the Vikings; the Cathedral of Mobile; buildings of St. Bernard College; the American flag, made from marbles, glass, and cement; and many more. Brother Joe's American flag is a tribute to the fallen war veterans of St. Bernard. There is also a Tower of Thanks, built as a way of saying thanks to his many friends who, over the years, sent material for his work.

Brother Joe worked at the Grotto until his death. Always modest, unassuming, and dressed in work clothes, he was often mistaken by visitors for a maintenance man. Sometimes they would ask, "Where is the man who built these miniatures?" Brother Joe would reply, "Oh, he's around somewhere. He lives at the Abbey." Brother Joe labored for almost fifty years in creating the park, and is buried only a few steps away, in the Abbey cemetery.

St. Bernard Abbey is the first and only Benedictine Monastery in Alabama. It was founded in Cullman in 1891 by a group of Benedictine monks from St. Vincent's Abbey in Latrobe, Pennsylvania. At one time St. Bernard included a high school, a college, and a girls' high school. There are now about forty monks, who keep up the grounds, the cattle farm, and the Grotto. They also operate the St. Bernard Abbey Retreat Center.

For more information, contact Ave Maria Grotto, St. Bernard Abbey, 1600 St. Bernard Drive S.E., Cullman, AL 35055. Phone (256) 734-4110, fax (256) 734-2925. Web site www.sbabbeyprep.org or www.alabamatravel.org/north/amg.html.

The Museum of Appalachia
A Mountain Man's Tribute to the Land He Loves

This museum is evidence of John Rice's love of the land, his love of his mountain culture, his love of the mountain people who came before him. One cannot walk these grounds and through these cabins without savoring the spirit and strength of a people rich in culture and heritage. You can feel them here, and this is the unique dimension that makes the life work of John Rice Irwin so extraordinary.

—Alex Haley

IT HAS BEEN MY extremely good fortune to have seen the great and celebrated museums of this world—the Hermitage in St. Petersburg, the Prado in Madrid, the Louvre in Paris, the Tate in London, and the Metropolitan in New York. Last spring I visited another museum—a different kind of place, another universe, a world removed; and now I find that my thoughts keep going back to it, time and again.

Nestled in a green wooded vale in Norris, Tennessee, a few miles from Knoxville, is the Museum of Appalachia. It is the creation, handiwork, and the heart and love of a remarkable man named John Rice Irwin, who has lived all of his life in the hills and hollows of this historic land.

Strong and sturdy men were born and grew up in the hills surrounding the museum: men like Cordell Hull, one of America's most distinguished statesmen, and Sgt. Alvin C. York, who is perhaps the most honored of all America's military heroes. Before moving to Missouri, Mark Twain's parents lived in a nearby log cabin that today is part of the museum.

A traditional farm scene at John Rice Irwin's Museum of Appalachia.

Photo by Starr Smith.

In the June 1986 issue of *Reader's Digest*, writer Henry Hurt wrote, "Deep in the Appalachian hollows of east Tennessee, John Rice Irwin has captured and preserved the very essence of pioneer America. . . . the Museum of Appalachia is truly a living collection. It includes pioneer cabins, a log church, a log schoolhouse—to name only a few of the many structures. Sheep, oxen, goats, and chickens dot the lush green pasture enclosed by rail fences. Throughout the museum there are some 250,000 relics, and in many instances John Rice can tell a visitor about the family from which the relic came."

I SPENT A SUNDAY afternoon with Mr. Irwin. He walked me around the sixty-five acres of his mountain masterpiece—the authentic log cabins, an antique shop, an auditorium, an extensive craft and gift shop, a large display building for the thousands of mountain relics, items, and articles, and the Appalachian Hall of Fame Building, which honors men and women of Appalachia.

Mr. Irwin says, "These are our people. World renowned, unknown, famous, infamous, interesting, diverse, different, but above all they are a warm, colorful, and jolly lot, in love with our land, our mountains, and our culture."

Mr. Irwin is a writer and author of seven books. He is also a man for all seasons—teacher, school principal and superintendent, college professor, musician, farmer, busi-

John Rice Irwin, in the dark coat, playing his mandolin with the Appalachian Museum Band.

Photo by Starr Smith.

nessman, historian, and, above all, the quintessential man of vision, enterprise, and entrepreneurship.

We wandered around the buildings and grounds, verdant and green in the springtime; past the rail fences, the freshly plowed fields, the mule-powered cane-grinding mill; past rooms where hundreds of old-time musical instruments are mounted on the walls, and other rooms where handmade tools, quilts, walking canes, carvings, gourds, and firearms are displayed. Then Mr. Irwin called together members of his Museum of Appalachia Band. Playing his mandolin, he led the band in a spirited serenade of melod-

Part of the museum's extensive collection of musical instruments, many of them homemade.
Photo by Starr Smith.

ic Tennessee tunes as true and pure as the crystal-clear spring water flowing through the grounds, and as toe-tapping as listening to the Grand Ole Opry on a Saturday night.

Mr. Irwin opened the museum in 1962 after spending years going to estate auctions and visiting mountain people in their homes, buying authentic mountain relics and other pieces for his collection. He says of that time, "It was my intention not to develop a cold, formal, lifeless museum. Rather, I have aimed for the 'lived-in' look, striving for, above all else, authenticity." It would seem that Mr. Irwin has succeeded in this quest. The official *Tennessee Blue Book* guide describes the museum as "the most authentic and complete replica of pioneer Appalachia life in the world."

Mr. Irwin began charging admission to the museum in 1968. Since then, visitors have arrived in record numbers from all fifty states and dozens of foreign countries, including faraway Australia. The museum journal indicates that on one October day alone, visitors came from California, Ohio, Kansas, Texas, South Carolina, Oklahoma, New Jersey, Germany, England, and Canada.

Mr. Irwin and the museum have been featured on U.S. television, in *Parade* magazine, *Reader's Digest*, and hundreds of American newspapers and magazines, as well as many foreign television/radio outlets and publications. The *New York Times* called the museum "a discovery of a way of life." The *Kansas City Star* stated, "It's the star-spangled banner from the country's pioneer past."

SO THE WORD HAS spread around the world about the pioneer museum and people have come, month in and out, year in and out. Word of mouth, Mr. Irwin says, seems to be the best publicity.

The biggest week of the year at the museum is Tennessee Fall Homecoming held in October. Literally tens of thousands of visitors arrive for Homecoming, recognized as one of the nation's largest and most authentic old-time mountain culture, music, and arts and crafts festivals.

Mr. Irwin says this is a sample of the week's Homecoming activities: Hundreds of old-time mountain folk; music and musicians with gospel, traditional, and bluegrass; dancing, including buck dancers and cloggers; more than 175 mountain craftspeople and artists; free parking; free cold water; sheep herding with dogs; log sawing and rail splitting; one-cylinder engines and antique tractors; a corn mill; well digging; a sawmill in operation; hymn singing in the museum church; and above all, storytelling and round-the-clock mountain music.

Plan to spend several hours at the museum. Be sure to see the Wilson Overhang Barn, the Main Display Building, the Hall of Fame, the General Bunch House, the Sharp Gristmill, and the Homestead Smokehouse. Best of all, just stroll around the grounds.

Contact John Rice Irwin, Museum of Appalachia, PO Box 0318, Norris, TN 37828. Phone (423) 494-7680 or (423) 494-1514.

Hotel Monteleone in New Orleans
Travel Home of Immortal Southern Authors

B ACK IN THE TIMES when Johnny Carson hosted the NBC *Tonight Show*, a frequent guest was the mercurial author Truman Capote. Not only was Capote—who grew up in Monroeville, Alabama—a brilliant writer, he was also a spellbinding storyteller who knew just how to put a shot of shock value into his narration.

One night, in a verbal sparring match with Carson, Capote casually mentioned that he had been born in a hotel in New Orleans. Like all good storytellers, Capote knew just how to blend a lot of imagination around a bit of truth. When Carson's eyebrows went up, Capote went on to say, to the delight of the audience, in his high-pitched squeaky voice, "Yes, I came into this world in the Monteleone Hotel in the French Quarter in the grand old town of New Orleans."

As was the case in most of Capote's stories—both told and written—he embellished this story from a simple fact: Capote's parents were living in the Monteleone when his mother went to Touro Infirmary for his birth. Still, Capote had a lifelong and sentimental affection for the Monteleone, from the time he arrived on a September morning in his mother's arms from Touro, right on through his luminous career, until the end came at noon in Hollywood on that fateful August day in 1984—only a month shy of his sixtieth birthday.

Capote was not the only great American writer to find a New Orleans home at the matchless Monteleone, there on Royal Street in the French Quarter. Tennessee Williams brought his grandfather, the Rev. Walter Dakin, to the Monteleone in 1958, and later that year William Faulkner arrived with his mother. To make the Mississippi triad complete,

Grand entrance of the Monteleone on Royal Street in the French Quarter in New Orleans—a hotel of the first rank, and colorfully connected with the South's literati.

Photo by Starr Smith.

Eudora Welty came down from Jackson, often stopping at the Monteleone. Sherwood Anderson lived at the Monteleone with his wife, Elizabeth, in 1921, before taking an apartment near Jackson Square, and the Pulitzer Prize–winning author Richard Ford was a Monteleone guest on numerous occasions. The noted literary scholar, French Quarter tour lecturer, and former University of New Orleans professor, Dr. Kenneth Holditch, likes to point out that the Monteleone's Carousel Bar is one of the settings in Eudora Welty's short story "The Purple Hat," and the Monteleone is in a scene from Richard Ford's "A Piece of My Heart." Tennessee Williams mentioned the Monteleone in "The Rose Tattoo."

I met Winston Groom for the first time at the Monteleone, shortly after the Mobile-born writer's book *Forrest Gump* became a phenomenal bestseller and an award-winning motion picture. When William Faulkner came to New Orleans to receive the French Legion of Honor award, he stayed at the Monteleone, and his biographer Joseph Blotner has said it was the Nobel laureate's favorite hotel. All in all, these distinguished authors have won four Pulitzer Prizes—Welty, Faulkner, Ford, and Williams—and the grandest of all, the Nobel prize for literature, was won by Faulkner in 1950.

Communications director for the Monteleone is the acclaimed New Orleans writer and publicist Bonnie Warren, who told me that another Pulitzer Prize winner, novelist Shirley Ann Grau, who grew up in Montgomery and now lives in New Orleans, likes to lunch in the Monteleone's Hunt Room Grill. Surely no hotel in the world—not even New York's Algonquin, with its celebrated "Round Table," has played host to more famous writers than the Monteleone. Indeed, in 1999, the Monteleone was named a Literary Landmark by the Friends of Libraries USA.

OVER AND ABOVE ITS colorful connection with the world's literati, the Monteleone is a hotel of the first rank—a sterling capstone in a bejeweled city. In my judgment, no hotel in town in any way personifies more the stylish verve and finely tuned New Orleans values than the Monteleone. Truly, it melds the harmonious spirit of the French Quarter with the elegance and sophistication of the Boston Club.

The key words here are experience and continuity. The Monteleone is among the last of the great family-owned and operated hotels. At this point, four generations of Monteleones have devoted their time and talent in the service of their guests. In 1886, the patriarch, Antonio Monteleone, an enterprising and successful bootmaker who had come to New Orleans from Contessa, Italy, bought a small hotel called the Commercial, which quickly became the Monteleone.

In the 125 years of the Monteleone's illustrious life, there have been six pivotal dates: 1903, 1908, 1913, and 1928, at which times rooms were added and remodeling took place. In 1954 the old hotel was razed and the foundation was laid for a totally new building—the present Monteleone. Finally, in 1964, Bill Monteleone, the present president and managing director, added more guest rooms and topped them off with a night club, bar, and rooftop swimming pool. Perhaps his most laudable move was to entice one of New Orleans's premier hotel impresarios, Ronald Pincus, to join forces with him at the Monteleone as vice president and chief operating officer. Pincus was formerly general manager of the Royal Orleans in New Orleans.

Today the Monteleone has six hundred guest rooms and suites, two ballrooms, three restaurants, in-house parking, a listing in the National Register of Historic Places, and membership in the Historic Hotels of America. An interesting sidelight for guests to know is that, early in his career, Liberace was a star performer at the Monteleone.

Just recently the Monteleone became the first hotel in America to receive the J. D. Power certification for providing "An Outstanding Guest Experience" based on service, total guest comfort, great rooms, quality food and beverages, value for the money, prompt attention at arrival and departure, and overall satisfaction. The great hotel remains what it has always been: a sparkling jewel in the French Quarter.

Hotel Monteleone is located at 214 Royal Street, New Orleans, LA 70130-2201, one block off Canal Street. Phone (800) 321-6710 or (504) 523-3341. Web site www.hotelmonteleone.com.

Jack Kyle and His
Mississippi Cultural Exhibitions
Tales of a Southern P. T. Barnum

O N SUNDAY, OCTOBER 1, 2000, the *Clarion-Ledger*, Mississippi's biggest news-paper, ran a front-page story—with a four-column photo—about Jack Kyle, executive director of the Mississippi Commission for International Cultural Exchange. Kyle is much better known in his more informal role as a dynamic and vision-ary impresario—an upscale P. T. Barnum—who is raising the bar on Southern cultural horizons and extending the artistic latitude for all the people of Mississippi and the South.

The tremendous and positive media attention created by Kyle's worldwide exhibits is also enhancing the South's image throughout America. In 1996 Kyle brought the *Palaces of St. Petersburg* exhibit to Jackson, and in 1998 came the *Splendors of Versailles*. These two widely heralded events drew 825,000 visitors to the Mississippi Arts Pavilion. The *Clarion-Ledger's* insightful story, by senior editor Orley Hood, is pegged on Kyle's current exhibi-tion in Jackson, the *Majesty of Spain*, which runs through August 2001. In putting together these exhibits—with stylish skill, ardor, and élan—Kyle has crisscrossed the Atlantic so many times that, as he told Hood, "I've worn out four passports."

It is Jack Kyle's modus operandi to bring the fabled treasures of the palaces, cas-tles, and museums of Europe to his pavilion in Jackson. In addition to presenting many priceless art objects for the Russian and Versailles exhibits, Kyle recreated entire rooms in order to show to Jackson visitors, literally and graphically, the lavish lifestyle of the Russian czars and the court of Louis XIV. He plans the same type of presentation for the Spanish exhibit, including paintings by Francisco de Goya, Anton Ming, and other artists from the

Glorious as the sun itself, a ten-ton twelve-foot-tall sculpture of Louis XIV on horseback remains in Jackson, a vivid reminder of the Versailles exhibit three years ago.

Photo by Starr Smith

Prado, along with cultural treasures from the royal palaces. Main attractions for the Spanish show are a golden gondola, a royal carriage, and the recreated Porcelain Room from the Royal Palace of Aranjuez.

This is the sort of broad-scale production that Kyle puts on—authentic, worldly, elegant, surprising, and always with a dramatic flair. For the St. Petersburg exhibit he recreated the Portrait Hall (with inlaid wooden floors) of Catherine Palace, the Yellow Hall

Dining Room of Peterhof Palace, the Throne Room of Gatchina Palace, and the Lantern Study of Empress Maria Feodorovna from Pavlovsk Palace. In addition, there was Alexander II's coronation carriage, a Faberge egg, and more than six hundred other art objects.

The *New York Times*, in its coverage of the Jackson event, described the Yellow Banquet Hall, commissioned by Catherine the Great, ". . . where bewigged footmen once served caviar on gold-rimmed plates." *Travel and Leisure* called the show "an extraordinary display of czarist treasures."

In 1998, when the *Splendors of Versailles* opened in Jackson, the *Montgomery Advertiser*, under the headline "*Splendors* is Truly Splendid," commented, "The mercurial Louis XIV of France, perhaps the most colorful king who ever reigned, made the sun his glorious symbol, and through the centuries he has been the Sun King. Now, in Mississippi, the sunny days of summer will welcome thousands of visitors to Jackson's Mississippi Arts Pavilion for Jack Kyle's eagerly awaited *Splendors of Versailles* exhibition." Kyle had another hit on his hands.

A huge floor-to-ceiling and wall-to-wall photo of the colorful Hall of Mirrors in the Chateau of Versailles greeted visitors in the lobby of the Jackson Pavilion. The exhibit included sculptures, musical instruments, clocks, paintings, tapestries, porcelain, jewelry, furniture, and carpets, all placed in a series of settings that vividly portrayed the Byzantine profusion of the Sun King's opulent times. The real eye catcher of the exhibit was a ten-ton sculpture of Louis XIV himself. The twelve-foot-tall equestrian statue has remained in Jackson, and is a striking and constant reminder of the Versailles run in the Mississippi capital three years ago.

Jack always puts on glamorous openings, and on that night the French Counsel General Jean-Paul Monchau of Atlanta told me, "I believe this is the first time in our history that such an important number of Versailles masterpieces have left France for a single showing." For his part in adding his imprimatur to the *Splendors of Versailles*, Kyle said, "The interconnecting histories of France and Mississippi date back some three hundred years to the reign of Louis XIV . . . Now France and Mississippi have once again united in a cultural exchange."

For his stellar work in bringing the United States and France together on such a high cultural level, Kyle has been knighted by the Minister of Culture of the Republic of

France. The Chevalier of the Order of Acts of Letters was presented to Jack by Consul General Monchau in a special ceremony in the House of Representatives chamber in the Old Capitol in Jackson in 1999. Only three other Mississippians, including author Eudora Welty and singer Leontyne Price, have received this exalted honor from France. After the investiture, in his typical breezy style, Kyle said, "Just skip the 'Sir' and call me Jack."

THE SUCCESS OF THE Jackson exhibits has posed a proper question, "How does Mississippi get great international cultural shows of this magnitude?" And time and time again, there can only be one answer—Jack Kyle.

I have known Jack as a special friend for more than ten years. A highly intelligent man, he has traveled the world over and is as much as home in Cairo or Istanbul as in Jackson. I have discovered that he has many interests, but only two passions—culture and Mississippi.

Margaret van Diest is a featured columnist for the *Ruston Daily Leader* in Ruston, Louisiana. She, too, wondered how Jackson, Mississippi, was able to get such dazzling

Jack Kyle poses with the Apollo clock from the Royal Palace in Madrid. The clock is one of only two in existence.
Photo by Starr Smith.

214

A majestic photo of Versailles's Hall of Mirrors provides the backdrop for Jack Kyle at a news conference in Jackson. Kyle is flanked by top officials from Versailles.
Photo by Starr Smith.

attractions as the Russian and Versailles shows. In a column titled "Now I Really Know— It's Kyle" that appeared in the October 27 issue of the *Daily Leader*, van Diest wrote:

> Having recently participated in the print-media tour to Spain with Kyle in command, I have seen firsthand how he operates. He only has one gear and that's Full Speed Ahead. And he only has one personal style and that's not First Class, that's World Class. One of the other participants on the tour who has known Kyle for decades referred to him as a magician. And all of this from a small-town Mississippi origin and upbringing. . . .
>
> How does he do it? First, he does his homework. He has about a dozen trips to Spain under his belt working out the details of the March exhibition, which is called *The Majesty of Spain*. The initial trips were made just investigating whether Spain would be a good choice for the project and meeting with officials who could make it happen. While he deferred to our highly educated, multilingual guides in Spain for details on the objects coming to the United States, they were deferring to him for additional input. That is about

Jack Kyle has made Mississippi a showcase for international art treasures. Here he stands before a carriage of the czar, from the St. Petersburg exhibition.

Photo by Starr Smith.

the highest compliment you can get. Second, he is one of those rare people for whom you just instinctively want to do your best. . . .

So, yes, now I know how Mississippi is doing it—it's Jack Kyle and the Army he assembles on his March to Perfection. And for those wondering if a spring jaunt over to Jackson would be worth it, just let me say that, rereading this column, the best description of these few paragraphs would be *understatement*.

KYLE IS A NATIVE of Minter City, in the Delta, and holds a degree in music from Delta State University at Cleveland. He says the school "introduced the world to me." And former Delta State president Kent Wyatt has said, "I know of no one who has done more for the arts in Mississippi, and for the national exposure of our state, than Jack Kyle. He's very loyal to his heritage and his roots, and that speaks a lot about the man."

In previewing the Mississippi exhibits, I have traveled to St. Petersburg, Paris, and Madrid with Kyle. I have seen him firsthand, interacting and working with high government officials, museum directors, curators, artisans, and even the laborers who actually packed the exhibits. He has an easy, compatible, smiling personality, a tremendous curiosity, a spongelike intellect, and formidable retention powers. He is "down-home articulate," in the Southern manner, and is the hardest working person I have ever known. His charisma brings out the best qualities in others.

The former First Lady of Mississippi, Pat Fordice, has said, "These exhibitions would not have happened if not for Jack . . . I've traveled with him and the Commission to France and Spain . . . and I've seen him persuade people to do the most extraordinary

216

things . . . In Spain the first time, he went in to see the director of the Prado with a newspaper article in his hand that said the Prado would do no more exhibits." The Prado made an exception for Kyle and for Jackson.

After attending Delta State, Kyle had a stint with the U.S. Navy in Washington and sang with the Navy's Sea Chanters. Earlier he had made a friend of Mississippi's powerful senator James Eastland. He said, "Senator Eastland had a reputation for helping people, and he certainly helped me." After leaving Washington, Kyle worked for an advertising agency in Memphis and later caught a break that would change his life. He went to work for WONDERS, the cultural organization that was bringing international art exhibits to Memphis. There he was instrumental in staging the Catherine the Great and King Tut exhibitions.

Buck Stevens, chairman of the then newly formed Mississippi Commission for International Cultural Exchange, got in touch with Jack in Memphis and invited him to Jackson. When his home state called, Jack was ready. The union has been an incomparable success, and Stevens speaks of Kyle in glowing terms: "Jack had a set of skills that we were looking for. He came and never slowed down. He's done a great job. He's put his heart and soul and energy into it."

Mississippi's current governor, Ronnie Musgrove, agrees. He recently said in a letter to me, "Jack has contributed a lot of time and energy in helping bring cultural exhibits to our state. His dedication and concern for the arts have given Mississippi the opportunity to enjoy several world-renowned exhibits."

Here I think I should mention a personal note. Before Jack left Memphis, I had gone there to cover one of the WONDERS exhibits. We met late in the afternoon and went to the Peabody Hotel for drinks. I found Jack so engrossing that, after a long dinner—with wine—we two old Mississippi boys finally said goodbye at midnight. We've been close friends ever since.

GROWING UP IN THE Mississippi Delta, Jack Kyle was not to the manor born. Early in life he developed a simple credo—"All of life is one door opening to the next door." In tiny Minter City, with little guidance, no museum, and no culture outlets, Kyle says that books became his cultural avenue to the outside world. He said, "To me, there's an experience with books that allows your thoughts and mind to go to different places. One of the most wonderful things my parents did was when they bought a set of the World Book encyclopedia."

Perhaps this heartfelt tribute to his parents and books helps explain a man who made twenty-seven trips to Egypt while working on the King Tut project. He also learned early and well the unparalleled value of cultivating the right contacts and influential friends. While working on the WONDERS Napoleon exhibit in Paris, Kyle made the initial and pivotal overtures that led, years later, to the Versailles exhibit in Jackson.

Yet even with a record of such impressive dimension, and with friends of stature all over the United States and Europe, mounting a major cultural exhibition still comes with myriad details, unforeseen problems, long days and nights, and the busy wings of butterflies in the nervous system. In his *Clarion-Ledger* story, Kyle pointed out, "There are so many factors—big investors, foreign contacts, visiting the country involved, selecting the pieces to be shown in Jackson, insurance, packing, shipping, unpacking, gift shop items, putting together a coffee table book, security, publicity, volunteers, and weaving all the various threads together into a seamless tapestry." Furthermore there is the mind-boggling task of revamping the interior of the Mississippi Arts Pavilion for each exhibit.

And after all is said and done, is it worth the ordeal? The mayor of Jackson, Harvey Johnson, Jr., apparently thinks so. He told Orley Hood, "First, the city gets out of it an enhanced reputation by having an international exhibit come to our city that is unique, one of a kind, and world renowned. During the *Splendors of Versailles*, magazine and newspaper articles appeared up and down the East Coast and across the country. You can't pay for that kind of publicity for our city. Literally hundreds of thousands of people come to Jackson to see these exhibits and, of course, spend money. We're very pleased that resources invested by the city have reaped significant benefits."

For more information: The *Majesty of Spain* exhibition will remain at the Mississippi Arts Pavilion through August 2001. For information, contact the Mississippi Arts Pavilion, Court Street, Jackson, Mississippi. Phone 1 (800) 409-9959.

The Little White House
Warm Springs Home of President Roosevelt

IT WAS PARIS IN the last days of World War II. Although the official end of the war was still about a month away, those of us in the Allied press group at the Scribe Hotel knew that the end was very near. Already the celebrations were beginning.

I was a young Air Force officer assigned to General Eisenhower's public relations/press staff in Paris, working with the network radio correspondents. CBS commentator Lowell Thomas had just arrived in Paris and I was his escort officer. I arranged for us to meet Charles Collingwood, the CBS correspondent based in Paris, at Ciro's, a private club near the Ritz Hotel. It was there I had the honor of introducing Mr. Thomas and Mr. Collingwood. The famous commentators had never met until that night.

Vincent "Jimmy" Sheean, the journalist and author, joined us, and across the room the celebrated dancer and American expatriate, Josephine Baker, sat with some friends. The club was crowded, there was dancing to a small band, and a gala evening was in full swing.

Suddenly the music stopped. The band leader came to the microphone and said, simply, "President Roosevelt is dead."

The band members quickly packed their instruments and in fifteen minutes the club was deserted.

THE EVENTS OF THAT long-ago and tragic night came back to me recently in a wave of somber memories.

I spent a reflective day at the Franklin D. Roosevelt Little White House and Museum at Warm Springs, Georgia. It was there that the four-time American president died on April 12, 1945. It was to Warm Springs, with its healing waters, that the future president had come in 1924, seeking solace from his devastating polio.

Perhaps no president has touched the hearts, the minds, and the sheer existence of so many Americans as the polio-stricken ex–New York governor who became president in the dismal year of 1932, when this country was in the throes of the Great Depression.

With his robust personality, booming laughter, endearing charm, compelling radio voice, deep interest in the welfare of the people, and intelligent approach to their problems, the new president set about restoring confidence and self-esteem to the nation.

Unfinished portrait—This portrait, which was being painted when the president died, is on display at the Little White House.
Photo courtesy of Little White House State Historic Site.

Speaking to the people of a country yearning for leadership, his speech made famous by the line, "The only thing we have to fear is fear itself," is considered one of the most inspirational of all times.

From his first visit to Warm Springs, on October 3, 1924, until his death there on April 12, 1945, Roosevelt made forty-one trips to the little village in southwest Georgia. It is not too much to believe that the soothing, healing waters, the tranquil life beneath the tall Georgia pines, and the fellowship and friendship of his neighbors did much to restore the health and confidence of a stricken man during the darkest period of his life.

After staying at homes of friends in the area when he came for his healing visits, he picked out a spot overlooking a deep wooded ravine for his own home. He moved in on May 1, 1932. The Roosevelts gave a huge housewarming party for the residents of Warm Springs, other local polio patients, staff members, guests, and cottagers. It is said that telephone operators were instructed to call residents in the entire nearby area and invite them and their friends to the party.

In November of that year, Roosevelt was elected president. His cottage in Warm Springs then became known as the Little White House.

The simple house was in sharp contrast to the large and stately home where the president was born in Hyde Park, New York, in 1882, and grew up. He was the son of an affluent and aristocratic family and attended Groton School, Harvard University, and Columbia University Law School.

Roosevelt was elected to the New York Senate in 1910, served as assistant secretary of the Navy in World War I, and in 1920 ran unsuccessfully for vice president on the Democratic ticket. In 1905 he married a fifth-cousin, Eleanor Roosevelt, niece of President Teddy Roosevelt. They would have five children, four boys and a girl.

Then in early August 1921, tragedy struck. While the family was on holiday on the island of Campobello, in the province of New Brunswick in southeast Canada, Mr. Roosevelt learned that he had contracted polio.

FOR CENTURIES, WARM healing waters had been tumbling from the rocky formation of Pine Mountain in west central Georgia. It was always at 88 degrees Fahrenheit, winter

The Walk of the States—This sidewalk, with flags and stone markers from each U.S. state, connects the FDR Museum with the Little White House.

Photo by Starr Smith.

and summer. Legend has it that the Indians came, some from far away, for the water's reinvigorating, curing values.

The legend of the waters spread.

In the early 1920s a young engineer named Louis Joseph, son of a prominent Atlanta family, contracted polio. His family sent him to Warm Springs. He arrived to take the healing water, low in spirit and in a crippled condition.

The warmth of the gentle waters prevented chills and the buoyancy relaxed his drawn muscles. Soon he was smiling again and walking with the aid of crutches.

In New York, word of Mr. Joseph and the healing wonders of Warm Springs reached the ears of the crippled young lawyer Franklin Delano Roosevelt.

Despondent and willing to try any remedy that offered hope, he came to Warm Springs in 1924. Roosevelt soon became a familiar and popular figure around the pool and, as he began to feel the tingle of life in his numb limbs, his jovial personality and booming laugh made him a welcome addition to the community of polio victims in Warm Springs.

Some have said that this was a major turning point in the life and times of this remarkable man. If so, it was also a turning point in the affairs of people the world over. Perhaps it was his own suffering that gave him such an acute understanding of the suffering of others. He was elected governor of New York in 1928, re-elected in 1930, and elected president in 1932.

FDR's Little White House—The house in Warm Springs where President Roosevelt died on April 12, 1945, is kept just as it was on that day. Roosevelt had the house built in the early 1930s. He died in the room on the left.

Photo by Starr Smith.

OFFICIALLY THE HOUSE is known as the Little White House State Historic Site and is operated and maintained by the Georgia Department of Natural Resources. It draws more than 150,000 visitors every year.

The house is the centerpiece of a beautiful and well-kept little park. A short distance from the house, and up a small hill, is the museum where visitors learn about FDR's birth, boyhood, education, marriage and family, public service, and days in the White House.

Well-displayed photographs and historic relics are placed throughout the six-room building that includes a small auditorium where visitors can see a twelve-minute film, *A Warm Springs Memoir of Franklin D. Roosevelt*. The film is narrated by Merriman Smith of United Press, dean of the White House press corps, who was in Warm Springs when the president died.

In this museum is a copy of the undelivered speech that FDR was to make to the nation. He died the day before its scheduled delivery. Here, too, is the famous Graham Jackson photograph, the picture of the accordionist who was FDR's favorite; the collection of walking canes; mementos from many countries; the breakfast tray used the last morning of his life; his monogrammed shaving brush, and his wheelchair and leg braces.

Visitors leave the museum, stroll down the Walk of the States, with its flags and stone markers from each state, take a left at the fountain and move between the Marine and Secret Service sentry boxes, then down a gravel driveway . . . and there is the Little White House.

It is white, much smaller than one would expect, and set off in front by four circular columns. It has six rooms—three bedrooms, a combination living and dining room, entry, and kitchen. A sun deck in back overlooks a deep ravine.

Leading off this deck is the tiny room where death came to the 32nd president on that fateful afternoon as springtime came to Georgia in 1945.

Essentially the house has been left the way it was when President Roosevelt died. There is the leash for Fala, his dog; a riding crop he used, and some of his ship models. In the garage on the left in front of the house is his 1938 Ford convertible, modified so he could drive it using only his hands. On the right is a guest house where many celebrities stayed.

The most memorable feature is the stark simplicity of it all.

In 1960, just outside the front door, John F. Kennedy made a campaign speech in his quest for the presidency, and in 1976 Jimmy Carter launched his race for the White House on that same spot.

The famous unfinished portrait by Madame Elizabeth Schoumatoff still stands in the living room, complete in all but its final details. Harold Martin, a Georgia author and the editor of the *Saturday Evening Post*, has written, "All that remained for her to complete a great portrait were a few more brush strokes. All that remained for him to round out a great and noble career were a few more years. The Creator, in His infinite wisdom, ended life and portrait together."

Contact the Little White House State Historic Site, 399 Little White House Rd., Ga. Highway 85 Alt., Warm Springs, GA 31830. Phone (706) 655-5870. Open 9 A.M. to 4:45 P.M. daily. Closed Thanksgiving, Christmas Day, and New Year's Day. Admission charge.
Web page: www.gastateparks.org/dnr/parks/allparks/index.cgi?mapval=all

Mobile's Bellingrath Gardens
A Floral Wonderland for All Seasons

HIS CAREER STARTED as a teenage railroad-station agent in the small south Alabama town of Castleberry, and when his remarkable life ended at 86, in 1955, the name of Walter D. Bellingrath was forever linked with honor and beauty all over the world. While still a young businessman, little more than twenty years of age, Bellingrath wrote to his mother, "By God's help, I am going to try to make the world better and brighter by my being here." Today that promise stands as a legacy to the world and a monument to his noble life. It is called, simply, Bellingrath Gardens.

Some say that spring is the ideal time to visit this vast and wooded floral wonderland. Indeed it is. But Bellingrath is the "Garden for All Seasons." In springtime more than 200,000 azalea plants in innumerable varieties and colors are an exquisite treat for visitors. The azalea, surely the South's own floral creation, is joined in spring at Bellingrath by daffodils and tulips. But the azalea, from giant to dwarf, reigns supreme, painting the landscape in a flood of vivid hues.

Summertime is the season at Bellingrath for roses, hibiscus, water lilies, crotons, copper plants, and other blooms. In autumn and early winter, millions of chrysanthemums are the stars in the world's largest outdoor display of multicolored blooms. From September to February, camellias line the paths of the Gardens with thousands of delicate flowers. But, just as certain Bellingrath aficionados believe in the wonders of springtime at the Gardens, many others think that Christmas is the best time of year. It is at this glorious season that more than ten thousand poinsettias cover the Gardens in a crimson tide of celebration.

Overall view of Gardens and Lake. I always feel a lifting of the spirit when I visit.

Photo by Starr Smith.

Bellingrath Gardens is located near Theodore, Alabama, about twenty miles south of Mobile. The best route out of Mobile is on Interstate 10, the highway west to New Orleans, which is 2.5 hours away. From Mobile take exit 15-A or 13, and the way to the Gardens is well marked. There is ample parking near the gates, and an admission fee is charged.

The Gardens cover a little more than sixty-five landscaped and well-tended acres in a wooded setting of almost a thousand acres. Bellingrath is also a bird sanctuary, with a wide variety of species. Squirrels, rabbits, raccoons—and perhaps a fox or two—also find a happy home in the Gardens. There are only a few places in this world where beauty has found such an ultimate dimension and magnitude, and Bellingrath Gardens, on small, sleepy, meandering Isle aux Oies (Fowl River) is one of them. I have always felt a subtle, almost ethereal, feeling in the Gardens. Perhaps it is a revival of the spirit.

IN THE BEGINNING, in 1918, it was none of these things. It was only a wooded haven slumbering peacefully in its natural state. Mr. Bellingrath, then living in Mobile, had made

228

a fortune as one of the early Coca-Cola entrepreneurs. He was seeking a fishing camp, a place of solitude and seclusion far removed from his busy life in Mobile. Toward the end of 1928 he wrote to a friend in Atlanta, where he had been born, "If a trade I am now negotiating goes through, I expect to acquire 25 acres of land on Fowl River near Coden, on which it is my intention to build a comfortable bungalow to be used as a country resort and fishing ground, and a place to entertain our friends when they come to see us." So it was that this tiny spit of land, which Bellingrath went on to acquire, and on which he built a fishing lodge called Bellecamp, became the fountainhead for the world-famous Bellingrath Gardens.

After coming to Mobile in 1903 and founding the Coca-Cola bottling company there, Bellingrath had married well. His bride was Bessie Mae Morris, daughter of a prominent Mobile family. While Bellecamp was originally planned as a male sanctuary, Mrs. Bellingrath soon got interested in the incredible landscape. She brought azaleas out from her garden in town and planted them in the woods near the camp. Soon the happy,

A profusion of flowers in the Gardens as seen from the terrace of the Home.

Photo by Starr Smith.

Bellingrath Home as viewed from Fowl River.

Photos by Starr Smith.

Bellingrath Gardens' Rustic Bridge across Mirror Lake.

resourceful, and enthusiastic couple had embarked on a program of beautification that led them, in 1927, to the great gardens of Europe seeking ideas to improve their Alabama paradise. Enter now a Mobile architect, George Rogers, who helped the Bellingraths fashion their wilderness dreamland into a garden estate, the centerpiece of which was a large and lovely house that remained their home for the rest of their lives.

Word soon spread of the beauty of the Bellingrath estate. In 1932 the couple opened the grounds to the public, and the future of Bellingrath Gardens was assured for all time. As the years passed, additional woodland was acquired, landscaped, and planted, until the Gardens reached their present size.

Now the Gardens are interlaced with appealing sub-areas—the Oriental-American Garden, the Rose Garden, Mirror Lake, Rustic Bridge, the Bubbling Pool, the Grotto, the Rockery, the Summer House, a Chapel, the Mermaid Pool, a Formal Garden, the Brick Patio, the Rebecca at the Well Pool, the River Pavilion, the Great Lawn, and the unforgettable Delchamps Gallery of Boehm Porcelain. Everything is interspersed with an endless continuity of flowers. All of these elements are interconnected with a well-marked walkway that allows visitors on a tight schedule to view the Gardens in a minimum of time. (Allow several hours for a leisurely and soul-refreshing tour.) I have always viewed Bellingrath Gardens not as a mere place, but as a state of mind to be savored and reflected on, long after the visit is over.

Centerpiece of the Gardens, and a magnificent magnet for visitors, is the Bellingrath Home. Built in 1935 of handmade brick and wrought-iron lacework, the splendid home reflects the cultural background, imagination, and remarkable good taste of Mrs. Bellingrath. The Bessie Morse Bellingrath Collection of china, rare porcelain, silver, crystal, and other priceless objects is on display. To be viewed, too, are the Bellingraths' individual bedrooms, the drawing room, the dining room (considered one of the most beautiful rooms in America), the Date Parlor, guest rooms, the upstairs Morning Room, a collection of English and French sterling silver, a Meissen urn, a rare "Versailles" centerpiece, and a wealth of antique furnishings. Since Mr. Bellingrath made his mark and his money in the Coca-Cola business, there is the Bottle Room, an engaging collection of artistic and utilitarian bottles.

THE HOME REMAINS as the Bellingraths left it; nothing has been added, little taken away. Mrs. Bellingrath died in 1943. Mr. Bellingrath continued to live in the home until his death in 1955. Shortly thereafter it was opened to the public. Both the Gardens and the home are owned and operated by the Bellingrath-Morse Foundation, which Mr. Bellingrath established before he died, in order to assure perpetual care and attention.

Bellingrath Gardens, with its unsurpassed beauty and worldwide reputation, is the fulfillment of the ultimate dream of Mr. and Mrs. Walter D. Bellingrath. Both are buried in a family cemetery plot in Mobile. Perhaps if they had been buried at the Gardens, their epitaph might have been the same as that of architect Sir Christopher Wren in St. Paul's Cathedral, which he designed: "If you seek a monument, look about you."

For more information, contact Bellingrath Gardens, 12401 Bellingrath Road, Theodore, AL 36582. Phone (334) 973-2217. Web site www.bellingrath.org. The Gardens are open every day of the year.

Beautiful Beaufort
South Carolina's Low-Country Jewel

O NE OF THE REALLY riveting things about the enticing little town of Beaufort, South Carolina, is getting there. It's about fifty miles from Savannah and seventy-five miles from Charleston. But if you are going from Savannah to Charleston, you don't go through Beaufort. It's out of the mainstream, off by itself—a principality without the prince, detachment without obscurity.

To get to Beaufort a visitor has to be going to Beaufort. It's not a way station, but a destination. After leaving Savannah, you make a right turn off Interstate 95 North onto a narrow highway and after a few miles you're in the storied low country of South Carolina—tidal marshes, swaying palms, faded rice fields, and moss-shrouded oak trees.

Then comes the town, on the Beaufort River: historic, stately Beaufort with the high bridge, commanding the waterfront, Bay Street and St. Helena Sound, Port Royal, Parris Island, and the soft breezes of the Atlantic Ocean.

I had heard of Beaufort, and heard of it as beautiful, most of my life. Now, late on a fall day, with the setting sun edging the waterfront, I was there. Beaufort anchors the south end of the low country, which stretches roughly 150 miles, hugging the South Carolina coast from Pawley's Island in the north.

Before night fell, I strolled along Bay Street and the parallel walkway along the waterfront, watching the fishing boats and pleasure yachts come in. The sun was almost gone now, and I watched a couple unpacking a picnic basket in the twilight, a young man walking his dog, and two fishermen casually trying their luck from lounge chairs.

I had the impression that Beaufort is a subtle town. I say subtle because there is nothing garish or flamboyant about the place or its people. I found civility, courtesy, and

233

Beaufort's lovely homes draw smiling tourists year-round.
Photo by Starr Smith.

politeness. After my brief stay, I felt that I had been courted in a gentle and stylish way. There is a soft mantle of contentment about Beaufort, and when you leave, you're glad you came.

Shortly after my visit, I was in Washington, D.C., where I met a highly placed young business executive and former assistant to a South Carolina senator. She grew up in Beaufort and her lawyer father still lives there. She has an interesting life in Washington, but says that Beaufort is not only home, but a heart-beckoning oasis.

As for myself, I found many reasons to like Beaufort and to yearn for another visit—the nearby sea islands, the river, the homes, the food, the ocean, and a way of life that seems to epitomize and burnish the hallowed reputation of the low country.

BEAUFORT IS AN old town. It dates back to 1514 when the Spanish explorer Salazar landed. Since then the area has been under Indian, French, English, Scot, and American control. It has a long rich history and a legacy of historic homes and grand plantations. Then there are the festivals, all tied to history and culture with music and storytelling. But Beaufort itself, against the backdrop of its magnificent homes, is the star attraction.

From my viewpoint, the single most appealing attraction in Beaufort is the old, well preserved homes that line the narrow streets and overlook the river—each with an interesting story. There are several ways to see these homes. Perhaps the best way is by guided carriage or van/bus tours. Phone (843) 525-1300 or (843) 521-1651.

I simply drove around in my car from one street to the next. That, too, is an experience in Beaufort.

One of Beaufort's glorious old houses was the subject of a story in the October 2000 issue of *Town & Country* magazine. The story, by the perceptive and clear-sighted writer Sarah Medford, told about Peter and Suzanne Pollack, a couple from Hilton Head, South Carolina, who had bought the house, which was built in 1787, and set about restoring it. As writer Medford tells it, "A few times a year they [the Pollacks] liked to drive over the causeway to sleepy Beaufort, cruise past the Chocolate Tree candy store and the mansion where *The Big Chill* was filmed, and window-shop for houses. One day, caving in to impulse, they bought one."

Later Mrs. Pollack, talking about her new hometown, said, "Beaufort has an amazing aura. In a way, I feel transported to another world, another time." After the renovation was finished, which took eighteen months, and the Pollacks had moved in, a New York friend was quoted by Medford, saying "The Pollacks are living in Beaufort because they

Still defended by cannon, this superlative Southern mansion, and many others, make Beaufort a wonderful vacation surprise.

Photo by Starr Smith.

like the neighborhood as well as their house. Well, who wouldn't? They have livable streets, kids playing, screen doors slamming—you wonder, 'What century is this?' "

Certainly, as a tourist town, Beaufort can't hold a candle to nearby Charleston and Savannah. Still, discerning visitors come, the subtle magic of discovery begins to work, and before the end of the day or visit, vows are made to return. Perhaps in a way, Beaufort really is in another century. And perhaps the shining moment of discovery is found in the noble, confident, and ageless old houses.

OTHER POINTS OF INTEREST include the Beaufort Arsenal, the Sheldon Church ruins and graveyard, Parris Island Museum, St. Helene's Episcopal Church, the Beaufort Museum, and the Thomas Hepworth House and the Elizabeth Hext House, both pre-Revolutionary, constructed during the Indian wars. The John Mark Verdier House (where Lafayette addressed the citizens of Beaufort in 1825) and the George Parsons Elliot House, which are the oldest houses in town, are now museums and open to the public.

One of the highlights of my Beaufort visit was a boat tour on the *Islander* down the Beaufort River to the Parris Island area. Phone (843) 671-5000 for information about boat tours.

Excellent accommodations are available in Beaufort, many of them historic. Some of the best known and most widely acclaimed bed and breakfast places in the South are in Beaufort. Among them: the Beaufort Inn, (843) 521-9000; the Craven Street Inn, (843) 522-1668 and the Cuthbert House Inn, (800) 327-9275 or (843) 521-1315; the Rhett House Inn, (843) 524-3177; and the Port Republic Inn, (843) 770-0600; I was very happy at the Best Western Sea Island Inn, (843) 522-2090.

The cuisine in Beaufort, which is outstanding, naturally centers on seafood. Try the Bank Waterfront Grill & Bar, a converted bank building, (843) 522-8831; 11th Street Dockside, (843) 524-7433; Johnson Creek Restaurant & Tavern, (843) 838-4166; Ollie's by the Bay, (843) 524-2500; or Hemingway's Bistro, (843) 521-4480.

The Beaufort city web site is www.beaufort-sc.com/beaufort.htm.

Louisville's Seelbach Hotel
Echoes of Fitzgerald and Gatsby

IN F. SCOTT FITZGERALD'S classic American novel *The Great Gatsby*, two of the main characters, Daisy and Tom Buchanan, were married in Louisville, Kentucky, Daisy's hometown. Daisy came through in *Gatsby* as a bewitching Southern belle of compelling beauty, a low sensual voice, and tantalizing appeal to men. Some have said she was drawn from Fitzgerald's own wife, the former Zelda Sayre of Montgomery. According to Fitzgerald's account in the book, Daisy "married Tom Buchanan of Chicago with more pomp and circumstance than Louisville had ever seen before. He came down with a hundred people in four private cars and hired a whole floor of the Seelbach Hotel."

The year was 1918. At that point in time, the Seelbach, built in 1905, was little more than a dozen years old, but had already become the focal point of Louisville's high society and had gained a reputation as one of America's most glamorous hotels.

Fitzgerald, an officer in World War I, knew the Seelbach from his Army days. Later, while working on *Gatsby*, and flush with the success of his earlier novels, *This Side of Paradise* and *The Beautiful and Damned*, Fitzgerald had poignant memories of the hotel. With his keen eye for elegance, it was only an extension of his own fashionable ways and stylish manner that the great hotel would find a place in his new novel.

The Great Gatsby was published in 1925 and came out to rave reviews that have been sustained over the years. Thus, being mentioned in the book has become a distinguished entry in the Seelbach's resume.

It is rewarding to know that Fitzgerald's timeless *Gatsby* and the mellow and stately Seelbach have grown old together, and each in its own way has continued to gain favor with succeeding generations. As one who has spent countless nights in hotels all over the

The Rathskeller at the
Seelbach. It is easy to imagine
Fitzgerald here, drink in hand.
Photo courtesy of the Seelbach Hotel.

world, I am drawn to the old places that have successfully, even triumphantly, met the vicissitudes and challenges of time, and the taste of new generations. I speak now of hotels like the Breakers in Palm Beach, the Peabody in Memphis, the Algonquin in New York, the St. Francis in San Francisco, the Monteleone in New Orleans, and the Seelbach.

JUST AS THE Seelbach has become, in a small way, a part of literary history in America, its history illustrates perhaps a larger place in the fulfillment of the American dream. In 1869, at the age of seventeen, Louis Seelbach came to Louisville from his native Bavaria and worked for one of the city's prominent hotels. In 1874 he and his younger brother Otto opened a restaurant, and a few years later opened a thirty-room hotel above the restaurant.

By the time the present Seelbach opened its doors in 1905, the two brothers were viewed as outstanding young Louisville entrepreneurs, and the hotel itself added a sophisticated panache to their growing reputation. With almost totally local financing, the Seelbach was constructed at the corner of Fourth and Walnut (now Muhammad Ali Boulevard), where it still stands.

Refusing to settle for less than the pinnacle of luxury, the brothers imported fine marble from Italy and Switzerland, bronzes from France, hardwood from the West Indies and Europe, linens from Ireland, along with Turkish and Persian rugs and carpets, special designs in china and glassware, and original paintings for all the rooms. The lobby featured writing tables, huge murals of pioneer scenes painted by famed artist Arthur Thomas, and a drinking fountain made from one of the largest pieces of Rookwood pottery ever cast. The Roof Garden, on the tenth floor, offered a panoramic view of the nearby Ohio River and the distant Indiana shore beyond.

On opening day and night the crowd was estimated at 25,000 people. Two years later the Seelbachs added still another gem to their crown when a new wing was built and the Roof Garden was enclosed. A German Rathskeller was created; Rookwood pottery was used to make the floors, columns, and walls of the large room, which was the first air-conditioned room in Louisville. Ten years later, 1917–1918, marked the time of Fitzgerald's visits to the Seelbach.

To be sure, the almost 100-year history of the grand old hotel has seen good times and bad. During one melancholy time, 1975–1981, the hotel was actually closed. But mil-

The lobby of the Seelbach. Flowers, columns, ornate carpets, and a grand stairway dazzle the eye.

Photo courtesy of the Seelbach Hotel.

240

The Seelbach's elegant front entrance, much as it must have looked when Fitzgerald wrote about it in *The Great Gatsby*.

Photo courtesy of the Seelbach Hotel.

lions of dollars went into a refurbishing, remodeling, and updating program, and in April 1982 the Seelbach reopened to wide acclaim and recaptured its former glory. In 1983 the Seelbach became one of only forty hotels worldwide to be selected by the prestigious Preferred Hotels Association.

The Seelbach is the hotel of choice for famous visitors to Louisville. Presidents William Howard Taft, Woodrow Wilson, John F. Kennedy, and Lyndon Johnson stayed there, as well as scores of other celebrities, including many Hollywood stars. A former Miss America, Heather Renee French, held her wedding reception at the Seelbach.

241

THE FINE-TUNING AND restoration of the hotel has been remarkable. The Rathskeller alone is worth a visit. The Seelbach today has 322 rooms with armoires, marble bathrooms, and other luxuries, all decorated in an eighteenth-century style.

The Oakroom features really fine dining, deep burnished dark wood paneling, and well spaced tables. It has been called "the most celebrated dining room in Kentucky" and has held Kentucky's only AAA Five Diamond Award for three straight years. More than seventy international publications have featured the Seelbach's Oakroom, and the hotel had a scene in the recent Academy Award–nominated movie *The Insider*.

The general manager of the Seelbach is Larry Hollingsworth, a Southern boy from Nashville who had previous big-time experience at Jim Wilson's Wynfrey Hotel in Birmingham and the Mississippi Queen in New Orleans. Hollingsworth says that running the Seelbach makes him "the luckiest hotel man in the world."

I spent a long weekend at the Seelbach. During my stay, I looked back on that earlier era of great hotels with fond memories and high favor. After dinner on my last night at the Seelbach, I went to spend a while in the Old Seelbach Bar. Listening to soft piano jazz, I, in my mind's eye, could almost see and feel the presence of the handsome and debonair Fitzgerald, sitting nonchalantly at the bar.

For more information, contact the Seelbach Hotel, 500 Fourth Avenue, Louisville, KY 40202-2518. Tel: 1 (502) 585-3200. Fax: 1 (502) 585-9239. Web site www.hilton.com/hotels/sdfshhf.

Steamboatin' on the Mississippi
Modern-Day Queens of the River

PERHAPS THERE HAS never been in the history of this republic a more elegant and romantic era than those times that marked the last years of the nineteenth century and the first few years of the twentieth. Much of this splendor could be found aboard the Mississippi River steamboats. They brought to America a new style and way of movement, carrying a message of grandeur and allure that helped to dispel the grim memories of the Civil War, and offering a beacon of hope to the newly reunited nation.

The steamboats dominated the commercial, economic, social, and agricultural customs of those times, putting the Old South in touch with the world, and ushering in a time personified by the rich planter, the Southern belle, diamond-studded gentlemen, and the riverboat gambler.

The rivers were the interstate highways of those tempestuous and explosive years, and life in the towns along the shore was a mix of adventure and excitement. Cotton was king. At one time more than ten thousand steamboats—some so lavish they looked like floating wedding cakes—plied the Ohio and Mississippi rivers.

The greatest period of shipping on the Mississippi was 1865 to 1900, the years that made cities out of towns like St. Paul, Minnesota; Cairo, Illinois; St. Louis, Missouri; Memphis, Tennessee; Vicksburg and Natchez, Mississippi; Baton Rouge, Louisiana; and, of course, New Orleans. Then the railroads came. Shipping traffic on the Mississippi River has never been the same.

Now there is new life and fresh excitement on the old Mississippi. It's called Steamboatin' and it has brought to modern America far more intrigue, romance, glamour, elegance, and convenience than the old days of King Cotton.

243

The *Delta Queen* (foreground) and the *Mississippi Queen* (background, on which I spent a marvelous week) bring to life one of the most elegant periods in the history of our republic—the era of the great steamboats.
Photo courtesy of Delta Queen Steamboat Co.

I spent seven marvelous days and nights cruising the river on the *Mississippi Queen*—a riverboat mate of the fabled *Delta Queen*, which has sailed the Mississippi since 1927. I found that Steamboatin' the river means getting away from the everyday world, savoring the good and valued things, and enjoying a rare experience that excites the imagination, pulls on the heartstrings, and brings back pride in the South's heritage.

The *Mississippi Queen* is a huge white paddle-wheeler operated by the Delta Queen Steamboat Co., which traces its river history back to 1890. Since 1946 the company has taken a leading role in pleasure cruising on the Mississippi and other American rivers.

During my days on the *Mississippi Queen*, I found that the paddle wheel is not an ornament, the steam is not a myth, the calliope is real, and that a generous, casual, and carefree lifestyle can be enhanced by superb food, excellent wines, a changing view, and spicy interludes of romantic glamour. And I learned that gentleness and hospitality were born on the river and still live a compelling life.

THINK OF NEW ORLEANS late on a fair Friday afternoon in spring. The *Mississippi Queen's* modern Robin Street Wharf terminal is to the right and upstream from where Canal Street meets the Mississippi. The *MQ* and her sister ship, the *Delta Queen*, are docked parallel to the boarding area.

Excitement is in the air. Passengers are moving slowly toward the boats, attendants pass out drinks and pralines, and a jazz band plays the old Bourbon Street songs—"Saints" and "Muskrat Ramble." And at the end they play "Do You Know What It Means to Miss New Orleans" as the sun sets over the looming Mississippi River bridge.

At 7 P.M. the "All ashore" warning has sounded; the great calliope on the aft deck just above the paddle wheel explodes in a farewell blast, and the cruise is under way.

Mark Twain, who got his name from the Mississippi, knew better than anybody that rivers were a vital part of America's heritage, the one common thread that held the nation together, and along which America began to grow. Twain would have loved the *Mississippi Queen*, called by its designers "the biggest steamboat the world has ever known" and "the grandest steamboat ever built."

The *MQ* was commissioned in 1976 in Cincinnati. It is 382 feet long, 68 feet wide, and 7 decks high. It was designed by James Gardner of London, designer of the Cunard

Line's *Queen Elizabeth II*, and built by Jeffboat Inc. of Jeffersonville, Indiana, where almost five thousand steamboats were built in the nineteenth century.

The *Mississippi Queen* has an elevator, Jacuzzi, sauna, gym, multi-tiered sun deck, beauty shop, movie theater, and library. The boat cost $27 million.

The hull and superstructure are all steel. There is on-board telephone and public address service, and individual climate controls in passenger cabins. The *MQ's* staterooms, cabins, and suites can accommodate four hundred passengers. All include a private bath, closet, room-to-room telephone, carpeting, and room service.

The boat has a grand ballroom and dining salon, as well as numerous lounges and bars. A versatile eight-piece band plays for dancing, tea dances, and the nightly floor shows.

Mississippi Queen cruises vary from three to fourteen days, sometimes even longer. On my seven-day cruise, the *MQ* made port calls at Natchez (twice), Vicksburg, Baton Rouge, and St. Francisville, Louisiana. These were usually from two to six hours. Bus tours were arranged to see the unique little river town of St. Francisville, the Vicksburg battle-field park, the splendid old homes in Natchez, and the bustling port, plantation homes, and state capitol building in Baton Rouge. (These trips were optional.) All meals were served aboard the steamboat, and passengers returned to their cabins at night.

MANY OF THE FOUR HUNDRED passengers felt, as I did, that life aboard the magnificent boat was the main attraction. Friendly bars with names like Calliope, Golden Antlers, and Paddlewheel encouraged good talk and camaraderie.

The *MQ* is a one-class ship, which means everyone dines in the main dining room, with an early and late seating. The boat's chefs present delectable food five times daily, including Southern breakfasts, hearty lunches, afternoon tea and snacks, gourmet dinners, and traditional midnight buffets.

Typical food included shrimp remoulade, prime rib, crab meat Louisianne, fried catfish, snapper, jambalaya, and Creole gumbo—and everything that goes with these dishes. Desserts, topped by an unforgettable pecan pie, were always on the menu.

A typical day on the *Mississippi Queen* might pass something like this: Watch the sunrise, eat a big Southern breakfast, work out at the gym, stroll around the decks, enjoy a full-course lunch, take a swim or sauna or massage, play bingo, bridge, or shuffleboard, enjoy port calls, relax in a deck chair and watch the river go by, see a first-run movie, fly a kite off the rear deck, take tea, enjoy the cocktail hour, have a big dinner with wine, dance to big-band music, listen to jazz banjos, ragtime piano, bluegrass, or torch singers, watch a minstrel show, and, finally, go to the midnight buffet. And then to bed.

The *Mississippi Queen* is a happy ship. The officers and staff, both men and women, have been sailing the river a long time. They are professionals. Moreover, they take immense pride in their jobs—to make the passengers feel more at ease, comfortable, and happy.

Some have said that the great Caribbean cruise ships learned the art of hospitality from the Mississippi River steamboats. I can believe that. After all, the river boats have been doing it longer. And the worldwide popularity of Steamboatin' continues to grow. The *Delta Queen* and the *Mississippi Queen* were joined in 1995 by the *American Queen*, now the largest steamboat afloat—all operating out of New Orleans by the Delta Queen Steamboat Company, which offers three- to fourteen-night cruises throughout the heartland of America and the Old South.

Mark Twain, who loved the Mississippi perhaps more than anyone, once wrote: "When I was a boy, there was but one permanent ambition among my comrades . . . that was to be a steamboat man." The great writer never realized this ambition to be a full-time steamboat man, but he wrote of the mighty river with glowing love:

> From Baton Rouge to New Orleans, the great sugar plantations border both sides
> of the river all the way, and stretch their league-wide levels back to the dim forest
> walls of bearded cypress . . . and now and then you see a pillared and porticoed
> great manor house, embowered in trees. . . . One cannot see too many summer
> sunrises on the Mississippi. They are enchanting.

For more information, write to Delta Queen Steamboat Co., Home Port Office, 30 Robin Street Wharf, New Orleans, LA, 70130, or call toll-free 1 (800) 543-1949.

Southern Scenes Gallery of Honor
Giants in Regional Tourism

IT HAS BEEN SAID that great things happen when people and mountains meet. Sam Walter Foss wrote in *The Coming American*, "Bring me Men to match my Mountains." If it can be said that the tourism and travel potential, goals, ideals, and purpose in the South are mountains to be conquered, then over the years seven great Southern romantic idealists have come forward with faith, vision, imagination, resources, and a compelling drive to forge a shining difference.

Today the Deep South is a peerless vacation, holiday getaway, and retreat destination, with alluring cultural attractions and magnetic family entertainment for millions of visitors, and an economic impact measured in the billions. (Indeed, the South is the home of the most popular vacation attraction on the entire planet—Florida's fabulous Walt Disney World.) Much of the success—the applause, cheers, and credit—for our region's success must go to seven people that I like to think of as the *Southern Scenes* Tourism and Travel Gallery of Honor. I must confess that this is a highly subjective list, based on my many years of observation and experience covering Southern travel, and with my personal knowledge of who they are, what they have done, and how they did it.

The accomplishments and deeds of six of these individuals have been heralded earlier in the pages of this book. Those six are David Bronner, founder of the Robert Trent Jones Golf Trail; Winton "Red" Blount of the Alabama Shakespeare Festival; Owen Brennan, Sr., founder of Brennan's Restaurant on Royal Street in New Orleans; Howard "Bo" Callaway of Callaway Gardens; Jack Kyle of the Mississippi International Cultural Exchange; and C. E. Woolman, founder of Delta Airlines.

249

Howard "Bo" Callaway, Callaway Gardens.

Photo courtesy of Callaway Gardens.

Jack Kyle, Mississippi International Cultural Exchange.

Photo by Starr Smith.

David Bronner, Robert Trent Jones Golf Trail.

Photo courtesy of David Bronner.

The seventh man, whom I would like to discuss now, is Bill Hardman, founder of the Southeast Tourism Society.

Bill Hardman, Southeast Tourism Society.

Photo by Starr Smith.

FEW MEN IN AMERICA, and perhaps none in the South, have painted on a broader canvas and with bolder strokes than Bill Hardman. He is now in restless retirement in a jewel of a city, Dahlonega, Georgia, that he helped to create as a beguiling getaway venue. From this vantage point, Bill Hardman can look back on a glorious career and see that, due largely to his efforts, a major region of the United States—the entire Deep South—literally changed before his eyes, in attitude, advancement, and accomplishment in the realm of tourism and travel. Truly no single individual has been more instrumental in bringing about momentous, paramount, and dramatic enhancement of tourism over a major part of the nation in a relatively short time.

Always the dreamer and innovator, in 1983 Hardman set about organizing the entire Deep South into a cohesive, coherent, and dedicated active force for the purpose of pro-

250

Winton "Red" Blount, Alabama
Shakespeare Festival.

Photo courtesy of Winton Blount.

Owen Brennan, Brennan's
Restaurant in New Orleans.

Photo courtesy of Brennan's.

C. E. Woolman, Delta Air Lines
founder, chairman, and CEO.

Photo courtesy of Delta.

moting tourism and travel. Thus, Hardman was the founding president of the Southeast Tourism Society.

He was ideally suited for the task. In 1959 Governor Ernest Vandiver asked him to develop a tourism program for the state of Georgia. Hardman agreed to undertake the project on a "temporary basis." In fact, he remained on the job as Georgia's first tourism director for twelve years, highlighted by establishing the Georgia Welcome Center program (the second in the Southeast) and organizing the first Governor's Conference on Tourism in America.

The Southeast Tourism Society, headquartered in Atlanta, with 450 members representing eleven Southeastern states, is the strongest regional travel organization in the United States. In 1997, after almost forty years in the tourism-travel industry, Bill Hardman retired as president-CEO of the Society, a position he had held from the organization's beginning.

ALL VISITORS TO THE South, and all of us who live here, owe Bill Hardman, David Bronner, Winton "Red" Blount, Owen Brennan, Sr., Howard "Bo" Callaway, Jack Kyle, and C. E. Woolman a large and sincere debt of gratitude for making our region such an exciting and hospitable place to visit and vacation. In other words, for creating so many of our favorite *Southern Scenes*.